Ascending with Ignatius

A 30-Day At-Home Retreat

Mark E. Thibodeaux, SJ

the WORD
among us®
press

Published by The Word Among Us Press
7115 Guilford Drive, Suite 100
Frederick, Maryland 21704
wau.org

24 23 22 21 20   1 2 3 4 5

ISBN: 978-1-59325-595-4
eISBN: 978-1-59325-579-4

Design by Suzanne Earl

Library of Congress Control Number: 2020918988

Made and printed in the United States of America

Acknowledgments

As this book goes to print, over 31,000 people from all over the world have tapped into the retreat, with newcomers still just getting started. Many of these thousands now consider themselves associate members of our church and they participate and pray with us regularly.

It's a miracle.

I would like to thank Tommy Krentel, who first gave me the idea for this retreat, along with the staff, the volunteers, and the entire community of Holy Name of Jesus Church and School. As your pastor, I feel deeply affirmed, loved, and inspired. This book is dedicated to all of you. I also wish to thank my brother Jesuits of the Loyola Jesuit Community for your unconditional love and support.

Finally, thank you to the huge new online community (HNJ-O!) who participate in our online Masses, retreats, reflections and events. We are privileged to have you as part of our community. Please keep coming back!

Contents

Introduction

Welcome to this thirty-day retreat, *Ascending with Ignatius*.

What Is a Retreat?

A retreat in the Catholic Church happens when we set aside a bit of time to be more intentional about our conversation with God. It could be a small amount of time, as small as a day or so, or it could be a longer amount of time. The maximum length is typically thirty days.

I invite you to spend the next thirty days as a special time. Devote these thirty days to spending a little more time reflecting on God and God's love for you. Talk with God, and let God love you a bit more. That is what a retreat is all about.

Ascending with Ignatius

Why the title *Ascending with Ignatius*? Back in the sixteenth century, St. Ignatius of Loyola founded a retreat program called the Spiritual Exercises, and you could say that he's the founder of the retreat movement, the patron saint of retreats. I have loosely based this retreat on his Spiritual Exercises.

Format

Each chapter contains between one and three recommended Scripture passages for you to reflect upon. Simply read one chapter every day for the next thirty days, and then spend at least fifteen minutes of extra prayer time reflecting on the topics in the chapter and/or the Scripture passage. You might also reflect on these themes throughout the day. Whether you're busy working or taking care of your children or whatever it is you're doing throughout the day, you can stop and reflect on the topic of the day. This will make it a full-time retreat, not just a fifteen-minute retreat each day.

I also recommend that you pray for the poor and the suffering of the world throughout this retreat. Perhaps you can even dedicate this retreat to the poor and suffering, for whom the Lord has a special love—a love in which we're all called to share.

The Spiritual Exercises

What are the Spiritual Exercises of St. Ignatius? For St. Ignatius, a huge part of the retreat is to follow along in the life of Christ, beginning with the Incarnation—with the Trinity's decision for Jesus to be born—and then moving to his birth, his adolescence, his hidden life, his ministry, his passion and death, and, finally, the resurrection and descent of the Holy Spirit. The Spiritual Exercises retreat is, as far as I know, the only universal retreat that follows the life of Christ in a chronological way. You and I, for the next thirty days, are going to be following Christ, accompanying him step-by-step all along the way. It's a wonderful way to spend a retreat—accompanying Christ our Savior.

Principle and Foundation

St. Ignatius says that before we even begin to think about Jesus' life, we must have a foundation. To build this foundation, two things must happen. First, we must reflect on why we were created. What is God's ultimate vision? What was his dream as he created everything, including you and me? We call this part of the retreat the "Principle and Foundation."

Second, we must reflect on humanity's response to God's vision. As you probably know well, from both the newspaper and your own experience, humanity's response to God's vision has been paltry on the good days and downright terrible on the bad days. Our response to God's plan for us often has been rebellion, disobedience, and sin. We need to make our peace with that. We need to spend a little time pondering this mystery of sin in our lives and speak to the Lord about it. St. Ignatius says that we can't go any further—we can't even begin to look at the life of Christ—until we lay this groundwork of why God created us and what our response has been.

Day 1

Principle and Foundation

Bible Passage: Psalm 131

Welcome to the very first day of our thirty-day retreat, *Ascending with Ignatius*. Here on Day 1, I suggest that we reflect on Psalm 131, which we'll use as our opening prayer of the retreat.

Opening Prayer

In the name of the Father and of the Son and of the Holy Spirit.

Lord, my heart is not proud;
    nor are my eyes haughty.
I do not busy myself with great matters,
    with things too sublime for me.
Rather, I have stilled my soul,

Like a weaned child to its mother,
weaned is my soul. (Psalm 131:1-2)

Amen.

Reflection

The psalmist says that his soul is like a small child sitting on the lap of his mother after having been breastfed. Imagine that child, probably the most peaceful little human on the earth. In a deep, deep rest, the child isn't thinking of things too sublime. He isn't thinking of deep and lofty thoughts, heavy philosophical or theological ideas. The child is simply resting in the arms of his mother. This is what I recommend you do here on the first day of the retreat. Place yourself in the arms and on the lap of our Creator. Seek to have the restful spirit of that child today, and for many years to come.

I was the novice director in a small country town in Louisiana called Grand Coteau, where I loved to go for runs out on a country road—Jack Fox Road. Jack Fox Road was made of gravel and dirt and lined with oak trees and pastures with livestock. There weren't many buildings or cars. About a mile into my run, I would stop and pet Sammy for a while. Sammy was a beautiful black-and-white Border Collie who was quite old. He would just sit there, resting his head on my leg while I rubbed him behind his ears and talked to him. This went on for years.

After a while, when Sammy would see me coming towards him, he would sit smack-dab in the middle of the road, waiting for me to get there. He became so used to this routine that when he saw me getting closer and closer, he would close his eyes and very slowly begin to lean. He trusted that my leg was going to show up right on time. I worried that someday my leg would not make it on time, and poor old Sammy would fall right over! But that never happened; my leg always made it just on time. With his eyes closed and his head leaning against my leg as I scratched behind his ears, Sammy was probably the happiest creature on earth.

About two miles further down Jack Fox Road was another dog named Smokey. Smokey was a small mixed-breed dog, much younger than Sammy. He was full of excitement and couldn't wait for me to get there. When I would arrive, Smoky would get down and lie on his back, with all four legs completely spread-eagled, so that I could scratch his little chest or rub his belly. I watched a nature video once that said that animals do their best not to expose their vulnerable parts to other animals because they might be killed more easily. Well, Smokey must have never watched that video. Lying there with his underbelly completely exposed while I scratched him, that dog was the happiest little creature on the planet.

One morning I woke up very early, as always, and sat for my prayer. As I prayed and sat in God's presence, I started thinking about my upcoming daily run. I thought about Sammy and Smokey and the Lord. And the Lord asked me a question that I will never forget. In my mind's eye, looking at Sammy leaning against me, the Lord asked me, "Mark, when are you going to let me love you that way? When are you going to close your eyes and lean on me and let me love you that way? When are you going to expose your underbelly so that I can make things well again?"

We all love dogs because they love us unconditionally, but I think we also love dogs because they receive love so well. We humans are not that good at giving unconditional love, but I would suggest that we're even worse at receiving love. And so, as the Lord asked me that day, I ask you today: When are you going to let God love you that way? When are you going to let God love you the way that Sammy and Smokey let me love them?

This is our task today. This is our mission here on the first day of our thirty-day retreat.

Choose some or all of the following suggestions to pray with:

- Reflect on the psalmist's image of a small child resting in the lap of his mother.
- Think about Sammy and Smokey and how dogs allow us to love them unconditionally.
- Ask God for the grace to let him do that for you.
- Ask God to make you the kind of creature that can receive that kind of love from the Creator.
- Close your eyes and lean into God's love today.

Let us close our reflection with the passage one more time.

Closing Prayer

Lord, my heart is not proud;
   nor are my eyes haughty.
I do not busy myself with great matters,
   with things too sublime for me.
Rather, I have stilled my soul,
Like a weaned child to its mother,
   weaned is my soul. (Psalm 131:1-2)

Day 2

Principle and Foundation

Bible Passage: Genesis 1–2

Welcome to Day 2 of *Ascending with Ignatius*. Before we can accompany Christ, we need a foundation. St. Ignatius lays this foundation with two reflections, the first of which we will look at today: How and why were we created? What was God's original purpose in creating us?

The texts for reflection today are the first two chapters of Genesis. These are quite long, so rather than praying over these chapters line by line, I recommend that you read the whole thing slowly and prayerfully and then do one of two things. One option is to choose a word or a phrase that you can zoom in on for some extended reflection. Select just a word, a phrase, or maybe a small sentence or paragraph. The other option is to set the text down after reading the two chapters and use your imagination to reflect on the themes I highlight later on.

The first two chapters of Genesis tell us the two stories of creation. Here we will read excerpts from the first of them. Let us begin this reflection by prayerfully taking in these inspired words.

Opening Prayer

In the name of the Father and of the Son and of the Holy Spirit.

In the beginning, when God created the heavens and the earth—and the earth was without form or shape, with darkness over the abyss and a mighty wind sweeping over the waters—

Then God said: Let there be light, and there was light. God saw the light was good. God then separated the light from the darkness. God called the light "day," and the darkness he called "night." Evening came, and morning followed—the first day. . . .

Then God said: Let the water teem with an abundance of living creatures, and on the earth let birds fly beneath the dome of the sky. . . . God saw that it was good, and God blessed them, saying: Be fertile, multiply, and fill the water of the seas; and let the birds multiply on the earth. Evening came and morning followed—the fifth day. . . .

Then God said: Let us make human beings in our image, after our likeness. Let them have dominion over the fish of the sea, the birds of the air. . . .

God created mankind in his image;

in the image of God he created them;

male and female he created them.

God blessed them and God said to them: Be fertile and multiply. . . . Have dominion over the fish of the sea, the birds of the air, and all the living things that crawl on the earth. . . . God looked at everything he had made, and found it very good. (Genesis 1:1-5, 20, 21-23, 26, 27-28, 31)

Amen.

Reflection

How and why did God create us? What is our purpose? There are two creation stories in Genesis, the first in chapter 1 and the second in chapter 2. These two stories were told by the Israelites. They were written during the time of the Babylonian exile, when the Israelites were invaded by the Babylonians and carried off into the foreign land of Babylon. Imagine them around the campfires at night. There was no television, no Netflix or internet, so the only entertainment was to stand around the campfires and tell their stories.

If you ask an anthropologist about a culture's image of God, they might tell you to look at the culture's creation story. You know a lot about how people think of God by the way that they tell their creation story. Imagine these Babylonians and Israelites standing around their campfires, and the

Babylonians start to tell their creation story. It is a wild and violent story of the gods warring with one another. One god kills another god, splits open his belly with a knife, and out of the belly come the guts. From the guts of this god come maggots, and from the maggots come human beings. This is the actual Babylonian creation story!

The Israelites are thinking, *This is terrible; this isn't how we know our creation at all; this isn't the God that we know.* So they tell these two wonderful stories that we now find in Genesis. These stories tell us so much about our original purpose, the reason why God created us, and the kind of God that we Judeo-Christians believe in.

This first story, found above, is written by the priestly author. We call this author the priestly author because it seems as though the author was from the priestly class and liked to talk about liturgy, putting everything into liturgical forms. This author wants you to imagine a great religious ritual: for them it would be in the Temple and later the synagogue, and for us it would be in our church. Imagine the most beautiful liturgy you've ever seen—magnificent rituals with gorgeous music, a huge orchestra and beautiful singing, processions, and vestments in a stunning church.

That's what the priestly author wants you to think about as he tells you the story of creation. He wants you to see creation as a beautiful liturgy with God the Creator as the presider. God says, "Let there be light," and light processes down the aisle into the nave of creation. "Let there be a dome in the middle of the waters, . . . every kind of fruit tree . . . , every kind of living creature." Each thing that God calls into being processes down the aisle in this beautiful liturgy that we call creation. It's a gorgeous image, and it's such a contrast to the Babylonian story that the Israelites were hearing.

The God of the Genesis story is in love with his own creation, not merely an architect over it. Though God is certainly a brilliant engineer and builder as he makes all matter of creation, he is also a fanciful artist. Only an artist would create little stars in the sky. God could have stopped after creating the darkness and the light and the dome of the sky and the earth. He could have created the sun and the moon, and that would take care of our needs here on earth. But then, like a fanciful lover, he puts in the little speckled stars in the sky. God does the same when he creates the multitude of creatures on the earth. Only a God who is fanciful and in love and having fun with his creation would create silly things like ladybugs and roly-polies! This is the kind of God we have—a God who planned out this creation and does it out of sheer love, exuding his very self into the creation.

If you imagine each one of these things being called into life and then processing down the aisle of this liturgy, you might think of a wedding. First, you see the ring bearers and the grandparents, then the court of honor, followed by the best man and the maid of honor. And the pinnacle, of course, is when the bride and groom meet one another in the aisle, and process down to the altar together.

What is the pinnacle of this liturgy in Genesis 1? God says, "Let us make human beings" (Genesis 1:26), and he creates humankind in his own image. This is when the trumpets blast and the timpani bangs the loudest—as humanity goes down the aisle of our liturgical procession. God keeps looking at his creation day after day, saying "It is good. . . . It is good." Do you think the Babylonian gods' humans coming out of maggots would say it is good? See the contrast here. The Israelites are trying to tell the Babylonians, "No, *this* is how we were created; *this* is the way humans are created— out of love, by a loving God, by a God who says 'It is good' of all creation, and of humankind on the sixth day, he says, 'It is *very* good.'" Humanity, as the pinnacle of creation, is very good. Then God sits in the presider's chair and rests.

The second creation story, found in the second chapter of Genesis, is very different than the first. For example, humans are created first instead of last in the second story. There are other differences as well, but what's interesting is that the God is the same. The image of God is the same image—fanciful, in love, and creating in a planned way. In the second creation story, we are introduced to God who is playing in the dirt! He's got dirt beneath his fingernails, and from the dirt, he molds and shapes humankind, breathing his very life into that dirt.

On Ash Wednesday, we receive the ashes and hear the words: *Remember that you are dust and to dust you shall return*. It sounds a bit somber on Ash Wednesday, but here, in that creation story, it's a beautiful image of a beautiful earth and beautiful dirt that springs forth life. God breathes his very self into us. Our life, the very breath coming out of our mouths, is the very breath of God. Truly we are made in love. We are made from a loving God who thinks we are very good.

Later, God sees that Adam is alone and lonely. Saying it is not good for humans to be alone, he responds by making us in partnership with one another. God creates us to be together with God and with one another. At one part it says that God and Adam used to walk in the breezy parts of the day. This is a beautiful and romantic image of God and humanity walking together. I'm from southern Louisiana, and I know exactly what is meant by the breezy parts of the day. August in Louisiana is hot and sweaty, but in the breezy part of the day, around 6:30 or 7:00 in the evening, as the sun is going down, it gets a little less oppressive, and everybody comes out of their own house and sits on the porch or walks along St. Charles Avenue. This is where you spend time, not with the people that you work with, but with the people that you care most about. So this image of Adam, Eve, and God walking together in the breezy part of the day is a beautiful picture of how God intended us to be. Here we find our purpose. This is why God created us: to be together as a loving community with God and with one another.

Later, of course, we hear the story of how humankind disobeyed. God goes looking for Adam and Eve in the breezy part of the day and can't find them. And because he loves

Adam and Eve, he goes out searching for them. When God finds them, they are hiding. Why? "Because we are ashamed," they tell him. And what does God say in reply? He asks, in essence, "Who told you that your nakedness was something to be ashamed of?" We often think that God is scolding Adam and Eve at this point, but it may be more like a mother who hears the story of her little child coming back from school after being told by a bully something that made him feel ashamed. The mother says, "Who told you that?"

Who told you that this is the kind of God that we have? God loves us so much; who told you that you should be ashamed of yourself? Who told you that you should be ashamed of your body? God loves our bodies. He looks at our bodies, minds, and souls and says "It is very good."

Notice what God does next. He sews garments. He loves his creation and is heartbroken that they're ashamed of their bodies, and yet they're stuck in their sin for the time being. And so, what does God do? God sits down and sews garments for them so that they won't be ashamed anymore. We see in this what kind of God we have. We see the purpose of our creation, the thoughts and the notions that God had in creating us. We see him playing in the dirt, creating the creepy, crawly things, breathing life into us, and saying, "It is very good" today.

On this second day of the retreat, I'd like to ask you to spend the day reflecting on all of this. God still looks at you and says, "It is very good." You are very good—your body, your mind, your spirit, your soul. "It is very good."

Let us close our reflection with the passage again.

Closing Prayer

In the beginning, when God created the heavens and the earth—and the earth was without form or shape, with darkness over the abyss and a mighty wind sweeping over the waters—

Then God said: Let there be light, and there was light. God saw the light was good. God then separated the light from the darkness. God called the light "day," and the darkness he called "night." Evening came, and morning followed—the first day. . . .

Then God said: Let the water teem with an abundance of living creatures, and on the earth let birds fly beneath the dome of the sky. . . . God saw that it was good, and God blessed them, saying: Be fertile, multiply, and fill the water of the seas; and let the birds multiply on the earth. Evening came and morning followed—the fifth day. . . .

Then God said: Let us make human beings in our image, after our likeness. Let them have dominion over the fish of the sea, the birds of the air. . . .

> God created mankind in his image;
> in the image of God he created them;
> male and female he created them.

God blessed them and God said to them: Be fertile and multiply. . . . Have dominion over the fish of the sea, the birds of the air, and all the living things that crawl on the earth. . . . God looked at everything he had made, and found it very good. (Genesis 1:1-5, 20, 21-23, 26, 27-28, 31)

Amen.

Day 3

Principle and Foundation

Bible Passage: Jeremiah 29:11-14

Yesterday we began to look at the foundation upon which St. Ignatius guides us to begin our retreat. Ignatius wants us to do nothing else until we've laid this foundation of knowing our purpose. I'd like you to spend today reflecting on Jeremiah 29:11-14. It's only three verses, but they are extraordinarily beautiful and consoling. Let us use these verses as our opening prayer today.

Opening Prayer

In the name of the Father and of the Son and of the Holy Spirit.

For I know well the plans I have in mind for you—oracle of the LORD—plans for your welfare and not for woe, so as to give you a future of hope. When you call me, and come and pray to me, I will listen to you. When you look for me, you will find me. Yes, when you seek me with all your heart, I will let you find me—oracle of the LORD—and I will change your lot; I will gather you together from all the nations and all the places to which I have banished you—oracle of the LORD—and bring you back to the place from which I have exiled you. (Jeremiah 29:11-14)

Amen.

Reflection

The words of Jeremiah were written while the Israelites were exiled in Babylon. The Lord was trying to console and encourage the Israelites by telling them that he has a plan, and it's a plan of goodness. It's a plan for welfare, not for woe. It's a plan with a future full of hope.

To help us reflect on these verses, I'd like to tell you a parable that is loosely based on a real person. Fr. Doy was a Vietnamese parish priest with a wonderful reputation for pastoral counseling. People sought him out and bared their souls to him because he was so gentle and kind. He always seemed to know just what to say and how to say it. Every gesture of his seemed to be just right.

One year, his parishioners gave Doy a gift of a thirty-day retreat. When it came time to take his retreat, his time with the Lord began wonderfully, with great joy and consolation. Over the first two or three days of the retreat, he experienced a great deal of gratitude. But around day three or four, he started having memories of a harrowing experience. As a refugee in his youth, he had traveled from Vietnam to America. It was a terrible journey on a boat, upon which several people died. On his retreat, Doy was being haunted by these traumatic memories—memories he knew he would keep for the rest of his life.

As these memories welled up inside of him, Doy found himself growing angry about it, even angry with God. Then, in his prayer time, the Lord began to show him something. Doy saw one after another of the people who had come to him for counsel, peace, and consolation. He saw that his own terrible experience in that boat was what gave him the ability to be present to others in their own dark moments.

Henri Nouwen once said, "The great illusion of leadership is to think that man can be led out of the desert by someone who has never been there."[1] But Doy had been through the desert. He had been through his own dark moments, and it became clear that those dark moments were what had given him the ability to be such a great counselor. Doy never talked about his experience on the boat with his counselees, and yet everything he did—every gesture, every smile, even every intentional silence—came out of his experience and his own knowledge of what it is to suffer.

God showed him in particular a couple who had lost their nine-year-old child and were going through the most horrific emotional and spiritual pain. Doy was able to be there for them. He gave them the ability to weather this terrible storm in their lives, and God showed Doy how he could not have done that had he not gone through that terrible experience on the boat.

Then, in Doy's prayer, he imagined God saying, "Doy, I know how painful and harrowing that experience was; I can take it all away from you if you wish; just know that I will also have to take away all of the good things that came from it as well." Doy thought about that couple whom he had helped through their own harrowing experience. He looked at God and said, "Don't take it away; leave it alone. Leave it be just as it is." And he also said to God, "If you could bring good out of that terrible experience, then I know you can do anything with any other moment of my life; and so, I give my whole life to you. I surrender my whole life. I give you a blank check, Lord. Everything is yours now. Do with it as you will."

I invite you to reflect on today's passage from Jeremiah. Try to hear in it the Lord's voice telling you, "I know the plans I have for you." Let him tell you that his plans for you are for goodness and for a future full of hope, not for woe.

I also recommend that you look back over your life and reflect on the good things that have happened. First, think of the great gifts and graces that have come to you, and give thanks for those things. But then, also look at some of the more tragic moments of your life, and see if you can't see what Doy saw in his own prayer. See if you can't see how God has made good from the terrible moments of your life. Perhaps, in a way, they're the most valuable moments to you, as terrible as they were, because they have made you who you are. They have made you the good person that you are today. Look back on your life, and see that God interwove these terrible moments of your life into his own great plan.

I do not believe that God brings tragic things into our lives. I don't think, for example, that God brought the coronavirus crisis. I don't think God brought Hurricane Katrina to New Orleans years ago, nor do I think God brought the horrors of September 11. I don't think God brings terrible tragedies into our lives, but I do know—in fact, I'm certain—that when tragedy strikes, God finds a way to interweave those tragedies into his great plan. The plan becomes bigger, stronger, and more expansive because of the tragic things that happen to us.

See if you can look back on your life today and notice that for yourself. Notice that the tragic moments in your own life have in fact led you to be a better person, and give thanks for that. Acknowledge that the Lord's words in Jeremiah are true for you—that God indeed has a plan even during the most difficult moments and the most harrowing experiences of your life. Find how God is interweaving those things into a grand plan to make you a better person. Give thanks and let it expand your heart. Let your heart respond as Doy's did: "Lord, I give you everything. If you can make good from these bad moments in my life, then I know you can do good for my whole life." Give the Lord a blank check. Let the Lord have your whole life today.

Let us close again with those very same words of Jeremiah.

Closing Prayer

For I know well the plans I have in mind for you—oracle of the LORD—plans for your welfare and not for woe, so as to give you a future of hope. When you call me, and come and pray to me, I will listen to you. When you look for me, you will find me. Yes, when you seek me with all your heart, I will let you find me—oracle of the LORD—and I will change your lot; I will gather you together from all the nations and all the places to which I have banished you—oracle of the LORD—and bring you back to the place from which I have exiled you. (Jeremiah 29:11-14)

Amen.

Day 4

The First Week

Bible Passage: Romans 7:14-25

On this fourth day of the retreat, we begin a new phase of the retreat. On the first three days, we have been reflecting on God's purpose in creating us. Ignatius wants us to begin this way so that we might have what he calls a magnanimous heart—a large heart. As we begin this retreat, he doesn't even consider this first phase the beginning of the retreat. He thinks of it as a sort of preamble to the retreat, which he calls the Principle and Foundation. It is this foundation that we are to build upon as we begin the retreat.

Today we begin what he calls the "First Week" of the retreat. By "week," he doesn't mean a seven-day period, but rather the first phase of the retreat. In this first phase, we still have a bit of preliminary work to do before we embark on the life of Christ. The First Week guides us to look at sin in our lives.

Our hearts are magnanimous because we have been reflecting on our purpose. But now, we are ready to begin the great race for Christ. We want to run the good race, as St. Paul says in the Second Letter to Timothy, but we have a problem. Just before we begin the race, we notice that there's a large pebble in our shoe. We must stop before we begin the race, take off this shoe, and remove the pebble. Otherwise we won't run the race well.

This pebble I'm talking about is our own experience of sin. We can't really go into the life of Christ with a free heart unless we've made our peace with our own experience of sinfulness. This is what we'll be reflecting on for the next several days. It is a challenging moment in the retreat, and so I ask you to be patient with yourself. Move slowly, patiently, and gently with yourself. Let us begin this phase of the retreat—the First Week—by reflecting on an excerpt from the Letter to the Romans in the New Testament.

Opening Prayer

In the name of the Father and of the Son and of the Holy Spirit.

I am carnal, sold into slavery to sin. What I do, I do not understand. For I do not do what I want, but I do what I hate. . . . For I know that good does not dwell in me, that is, in my flesh. The willing is ready at hand, but doing the good is not. For I do not do the good I want, but I do the evil I do not want. . . . For I take delight in the law of God, in my inner self, but I see in my members another principle at war with the law of my mind, taking me captive to the law of sin that dwells in my members. Miserable one that I am! Who will deliver me? (Romans 7:14-15, 18-19, 22-24)

Amen.

Reflection

Today I ask you to do the sober and difficult task of looking at your own personal experience of sin. What has been your experience of sin? What has been your negative response to God's ultimate vision for you?

I recommend you look at four aspects of sin today.

First, I recommend that as you think about the list of your sins—the things that you've done wrong throughout your life that have kept you from living according to the will of God—pick the one that bothers you the most. Spend a little time reflecting and speaking with the Lord about the sin that bothers you the most.

Second, look at God's pick. What do I mean? When we examine our sins, we have the usual suspects—the things that we tend to go to again and again. Once we've looked at them for a little while, we've probably picked those bones pretty clean. But perhaps we can put those usual suspects aside for a moment. Let's ask God, "Which one bothers you the most,

Lord?" You may find to your surprise that there's a sin that doesn't bother you very much but that bothers God quite a bit. That's the second thing we do today.

Third, what are our sins of omission? When we examine our consciences, we often tend to look more at the things that we've done wrong. Perhaps, as we get more mature in the spiritual life, we don't do so many acts of sin. We might notice, rather, sins of omission. These are things that we could do but we've neglected to do. What sin of omission comes to mind as you reflect?

Fourth and finally, we want to look at the root of our sinfulness. What is the root cause of our sinfulness? When we go into the confessional, we tend to list off our sinful behaviors. That is appropriate, but we should also spend a bit of time asking ourselves about what is underneath the sin. What is it that is causing us to do these sinful behaviors? What has led us to these sinful paths?

There's a parable about a little village in a small town. A man is walking along a beautiful stream in his small village, and he sees a baby floating in the river. Terrified, he jumps into the river to rescue the baby. Other villagers come to help, taking the baby to safety. The next day the same man is walking along the river, and this time he sees two babies floating in the river. He jumps back into the river again, rescuing both babies. More townspeople come to help them out. The next day there are four babies in the river. He and others all start jumping in the river to save these babies. The next day it's eight, and the next day it's sixteen babies floating in the river, and all of these townspeople are working hard to help. They are trying their hardest to rescue all of these babies floating down the river, when finally, there in a quiet moment after scooping up that day's batch of babies, someone asks, "Why don't we send someone up the river to find out who's putting all these babies in the river?"

It's a wonderful metaphor for our own sinful behavior. If my sin is that I have angrily snapped at someone, I need to ask God for forgiveness for that sin. But I might also want to spend time asking myself and the Lord: What is the root of that anger? Where does that anger come from? Who threw the baby "Anger" into the river? How did it come to be that my disposition was angry? If we only spend time looking at the sinful behaviors themselves, then we will never get to the place upriver in our spiritual lives, to the place where the baby is first thrown into the river. Choose a sinful pattern in your life and take a mental journey upriver in prayer. What do you discover up there?

These four angles on sin are difficult to look at, painful even. And of course, you want to do it in God's presence and Spirit. You want to ask the Lord to lead you through it all. Never forget that you are indeed forgiven for your sins and that you are loved by God. We look at our sins, not to beat ourselves up about them but, rather, so that we may know truly who we are in order to take our sinful selves to the Lord. We do this exercise so that the Lord can forgive us and that we might, once again, experience the great mercy of God.

To review, today you'll be looking at four things:

1. Identify a sin that most bothers you.
2. Look for God's pick, asking the Lord to show you what behavior bothers him the most.
3. Look at your sins of omission—the things that you've neglected to do.
4. Perhaps most importantly, what is the root of your sinful behavior? Where does it come from? Why have you sinned in the first place?

Let us conclude our session today by reflecting once again on our passage from St. Paul.

Closing Prayer

I am carnal, sold into slavery to sin. What I do, I do not understand. For I do not do what I want, but I do what I hate. . . . For I know that good does not dwell in me, that is, in my flesh. The willing is ready at hand, but doing the good is not. For I do not do the good I want, but I do the evil I do not want. . . . For I take delight in the law of God, in my inner self, but I see in my members another principle at war with the law of my mind, taking me captive to the law of sin that dwells in my members. Miserable one that I am! Who will deliver me? (Romans 7:14-15, 18-19, 22-24)

Amen.

Day 5

The First Week

Bible Passage: Psalm 51

Welcome to Day 5 of *Ascending with Ignatius*. We are still in what Ignatius calls the First Week, reflecting on our own experience of sin and mercy. Yesterday I gave you quite a difficult homework assignment, a sober and painful one. I instructed you to first look over the sins of your past and ask yourself which sin you would like to choose to discuss with God. Which one bothers you the most? Second, you let God pick the one that bothers him the most; maybe it was something you weren't expecting. Third, I asked you to reflect on your experience of the sin of omission—not what wrong thing you have done but what right thing you've failed to do. Fourth, and perhaps the biggest and the most difficult challenge of all, was to go upriver and get some insight on the root of your sin.

You could spend thirty days reflecting only on these four prompts, and I've only given you twenty-four hours to get started. So we are going to continue the First Week for several days. Here on this second day of the First Week of the retreat, I ask you to continue reflecting on the four prompts from yesterday: your pick, God's pick, sins of omission, and the root of your sin.

In addition to the four prompts, I'd simply like to add a question to ponder. It's not a fifth assignment but something to keep in mind as you go forward in reflecting on those four prompts. We'll get to the question at the end of this reflection, but let us begin by using an excerpt from Psalm 51 as our opening prayer today.

Opening Prayer

In the name of the Father and of the Son and of the Holy Spirit.

Have mercy on me, God, in accord with your merciful love;
    in your abundant compassion blot out my transgressions.
Thoroughly wash away my guilt;
    and from my sin cleanse me.
For I know my transgressions;
    my sin is always before me.
Against you, you alone have I sinned;
    I have done what is evil in your eyes. . . .

Behold, you desire true sincerity;

    and secretly you teach me wisdom.

Cleanse me with hyssop, that I may be pure;

    wash me, and I will be whiter than snow. (Psalm 51:3-6, 8-9)

Amen.

Reflection

I was eighteen years old when I first joined the Jesuits. After about a year in the order, all novices are asked to fill out a form called an *informatio*, equivalent to an employee evaluation in the secular world. In it, you are asked to let the leadership of the Jesuits know the strengths and weaknesses of a fellow Jesuit, presumably someone that you know well. The purpose of these *informatios* is to help the Society of Jesus determine where they might mission this Jesuit and how they might help him to grow.

There are different forms of this *informatio*, but the one that we received opened with a question that I remember to this day. The question was: "Does this man, your brother novice, know himself to be a sinner, loved and redeemed by God?" A sinner loved and redeemed by God. As a nineteen-year-old, I was really struck by that question and wondered why on earth that would be the first question that the Society of Jesus would want to know about my brother Jesuit. I would have thought they would have asked if this man is holy enough or smart enough or competent enough. Does he obey the rules? But what they wanted to know, first and foremost, was whether or not this man experiences himself as a sinner, loved and redeemed by God.

I have since learned that this phrase—"sinner loved and redeemed by God"—is an important phrase for the Jesuits. Jesuits all around the world know it and speak of this as an important part of our identity. Jorge Bergoglio—in his very first interview as Pope Francis, was asked the question: "Who is Jorge Bergoglio?" The new pope smiled and said, "Jorge Bergoglio is a sinner." The whole world gasped, thinking that he was going to do some exposé of himself, that he had some secret sin he was about to reveal. But all the Jesuits around the world just smiled because we knew that this is the answer that a Jesuit gives when asked about his identity: a sinner loved and redeemed by God. That's how we Jesuits think of ourselves, first and foremost.

This balance of "sinner loved and redeemed by God" is very important to us. It's important to keep these two things balanced. If you know yourself to be a sinner, but you don't know yourself to be loved and redeemed by God, then you will be filled with self-loathing, and you will be of no use to the Lord. A person who is filled with self-loathing, who doesn't like himself or herself, will not be a very effective apostle.

But it's also a problem if you know yourself loved and redeemed by God, but you don't know yourself as a sinner. First and foremost, this can lead to a lack of humility. St. Ignatius says that humility is the foundation of all virtue, and a lack of humility is the root of all sin, so humility is an extremely important virtue that we should be striving and praying for. A lack of humility also leads you to moral superiority, which in turn leads you to a host of other problems.

Another consequence of not knowing yourself as a sinner is not knowing of your own capacity to hurt other people. The fact that I know myself as a sinner makes me cautious. It helps me realize that when I'm with someone else, I am always in danger of hurting them. I know that from my own experience of sin, and so it makes me better at loving others.

We must therefore keep this balance between knowing ourselves as sinners and knowing ourselves as loved and redeemed by God. Catholics who grew up before Vatican II sometimes get stuck on the sinner part and don't know well enough that they are loved and redeemed by God. The younger generation, those born after the 1970s, often know themselves to be loved and redeemed by God but may not be quite as aware, deep down in their hearts, of their own sinfulness.

As you are working on your four reflection assignments from yesterday, I'd like to ask you to ponder this question as well—do you have this balance between knowing yourself as loved and redeemed and as a sinner? Are you well-balanced in the knowledge of both of these things? If not, which one are you lacking? Do you lack this knowledge of your own sinfulness? Then ask the Lord to give you a knowledge of your sinfulness. Are you too much aware of your sinfulness and filled with self-loathing? Then ask the Lord to give you the grace of knowing just how much he loves you and that you are redeemed—completely and divinely redeemed.

Let us close today with that same passage from Psalm 51.

Closing Prayer

Have mercy on me, God, in accord with your merciful love;
　　in your abundant compassion blot out my transgressions.
Thoroughly wash away my guilt;
　　and from my sin cleanse me.
For I know my transgressions;
　　my sin is always before me.
Against you, you alone have I sinned;
　　I have done what is evil in your eyes. . . .
Behold, you desire true sincerity;
　　and secretly you teach me wisdom.
Cleanse me with hyssop, that I may be pure;
　　wash me, and I will be whiter than snow. (Psalm 51:3-6, 8-9)

Amen.

Day 6

The First Week

Bible Passage: Psalm 103

Welcome to Day 6. We are in the middle of the first phase of the retreat that St. Ignatius calls the First Week, and we've been reflecting on the reality of sin and mercy in our lives. We are in the midst of examining our own conscience, looking at our sinfulness. We do this, not to beat ourselves up about it or to fall into self-loathing, but so that we can truly come to the Lord with repentant hearts and allow the Lord to forgive us of our sins.

Today I'd like you to take a little bit of a shift. For the last two days, we have been taking a sober look at the things that we've done wrong. Today I'd like you to start to reflect on the Lord forgiving you of your sins and on you forgiving yourself. Today I'm going to challenge you to reflect on this question:

- Is there anything for which you haven't yet forgiven yourself?

And if so,

- Might you take this retreat as an opportunity to finally forgive yourself for your own personal unforgivable sin?

Today's Scripture passage is from Psalm 103. Let's begin with praying this psalm.

Opening Prayer

In the name of the Father and of the Son and of the Holy Spirit.

Bless the LORD, my soul;
    all my being, bless his holy name!
Bless the LORD, my soul;
    and do not forget all his gifts,
Who pardons all your sins,
    and heals all your ills,
Who redeems your life from the pit,
    and crowns you with mercy and compassion,
Who fills your days with good things,
    so your youth is renewed like the eagle's. . . .

He made known his ways to Moses,
  to the Israelites his deeds.
Merciful and gracious is the LORD,
  slow to anger, abounding in mercy.
He will not always accuse,
  and nurses no lasting anger;
He has not dealt with us as our sins merit,
  nor requited us as our wrongs deserve.

For as the heavens tower over the earth,
  so his mercy towers over those who fear him. (Psalm 103:1-5, 7-11)

Amen.

Reflection

Today I'd like you to reflect on the question of your own forgiveness. We of course want to turn to the Lord and ask him for forgiveness, and you could begin to do that today if you haven't already started. Around this time in the retreat, if you are able to go to Confession, I highly recommend that.

But I also want to ask you: have you forgiven yourself?

There's a strange passage in the Gospels where Jesus says that all sins will be forgiven except for one: the sin against the Holy Spirit (see Mark 3:29). That's all he says. What did Jesus mean by the sin against the Holy Spirit? We don't exactly know. No one really knows, and scholars have debated this for centuries.

Everyone agrees, however, about what these words don't mean. They do not mean that the Lord can't forgive you, because the Lord can forgive any sin. The Lord is more powerful than our greatest sins. I'm not as concerned about what *the* unforgivable sin is; I'm more concerned about what *your* unforgivable sin is. In other words, what is the sin that you have decided is simply unforgivable? Perhaps you've forgiven yourself for this sin here, that sin there, and that other one over there, but there's one sin that you've never forgiven yourself for. As a priest for so many years, I know this for a fact now: many people—not everyone, but so many people—are carrying around an "unforgivable sin" in their hearts. So I want to ask you today, what is your unforgivable sin? What is the sin that you have not freed yourself of?

In the case of this unforgivable sin, it's not a matter of Christ forgiving you. It's a matter of you forgiving yourself. Christ has been waiting to forgive you for so long and has been waiting for you to give him consent. Perhaps this is precisely what Jesus meant by the unforgivable sin—that he cannot forgive a sin until you give him permission to do so. And so, why don't you use this retreat to do so? Why not use this moment to let yourself forgive yourself? Finally unburden yourself of that weight, of what you thought was unforgivable, and give it back to God.

It's understandable that we would be so hard on ourselves when we sin. It's understandable that we don't want to forgive ourselves because we know well the permanency of our sins. We know the terrible damage our sins do in the world, and the truth is we can't ever make up for our sins. We can't ever make it right again.

There is a parable of a woman who went to Confession to her small-town priest and confessed the sin of gossip. She didn't seem very sorry while confessing it, so the priest gave her a very unusual penance. "Before I give you absolution," he said, "you need to go and buy yourself a pillow. Split the pillow open and walk around town waving this pillow in the air until all of the little feathers fly all around the town. Then, come back and see me."

So the woman did just that. She split open the pillow, walked and waved it all around town as the feathers flew in every direction. Coming back to the priest, she said, "Okay, I'm ready now. Can I have my absolution?"

And the priest said, "You now have only one other thing to do. Go and gather up all of those feathers."

The woman knew there was no way she would ever be able to do that. And she also knew what the priest was getting at. The sin of gossip, and all of our sins really, are completely irretrievable. Once we sin, the damage is in the world permanently—at least this side of heaven. It's understandable that we would have such a hard time forgiving ourselves, and yet that is in fact our calling.

Have you ever had the following experience? You snap at someone you love, who is a wonderful person. Or you betray them in some way or do something harsh to them. You go to them and say you're sorry, and they forgive you. But you don't feel better at first; you feel even worse. At least sometimes, that forgiveness that we get from such a loving person that we've hurt is a bit painful for us. We sometimes feel the pain even of forgiveness.

When someone comes to me and confesses a sin that they feel so horrible about, their own unforgivable sin, I find myself giving a smaller penance. The graver the sin, the smaller the penance, because the true penance of every sin is having to live with the forgiveness. It's difficult. It's painful to allow ourselves to be forgiven.

This is what the Lord is demanding that we do. The Lord demands that we bring our sins to him so that he can heal us and make us whole again. Won't you do that today? Won't you finally take those sins, and especially that unforgivable sin, back to the Lord? Give it to him and let him finally forgive you. I often call the Sacrament of Confession the sacrament of giving God permission to forgive us. God has been waiting for you to give him permission to forgive you of the unforgivable sin.

Let us close with that same passage from Psalm 103.

Closing Prayer

Bless the LORD, my soul;
   all my being, bless his holy name!
Bless the LORD, my soul;
   and do not forget all his gifts,
Who pardons all your sins,
   and heals all your ills,
Who redeems your life from the pit,
   and crowns you with mercy and compassion,
Who fills your days with good things,
   so your youth is renewed like the eagle's. . . .

He made known his ways to Moses,
   to the Israelites his deeds.
Merciful and gracious is the LORD,
   slow to anger, abounding in mercy.
He will not always accuse,
   and nurses no lasting anger;
He has not dealt with us as our sins merit,
   nor requited us as our wrongs deserve.

For as the heavens tower over the earth,
   so his mercy towers over those who fear him. (Psalm
103:1-5, 7-11)

Amen.

Day 7

The First Week

Bible Passage: Luke 15:11-32

Welcome to Day 7 of *Ascending with Ignatius*. We are now on the very last day of the First Week of this retreat based on the Spiritual Exercises. Today we conclude the retreat's first movement in which we reflect on our sin and the mercy of God. For the last several days, I've challenged you to take a sober look at your own experience of sin. I've challenged you to go to those difficult places in your soul, to really look hard and make your peace with the fact that you have sinned. Today, on the last day of the First Week, we are called to rejoice by celebrating our forgiveness. We celebrate the fact that God's love and mercy overwhelm—even steamroll—our sins! It is a day of jubilation.

We begin our session today as always with a little prayer from Scripture. I invite you to reflect on the much beloved story of the prodigal son in Luke 15:11-32. Let us begin with the very last line of that parable where the father is speaking with the elder son.

Opening Prayer

In the name of the Father and of the Son and of the Holy Spirit.

But now we must celebrate and rejoice, because our brother was dead and has come to life again; he was lost and has been found. (Luke 15:32)

Amen.

Reflection

A few days back, I explained that an important aspect of Jesuit identity is to know oneself as a sinner loved and redeemed by God. Today I want to say a bit more about why this is so important for Jesuits. It is because of our experience of the First Week in the Spiritual Exercises.

All Jesuits have an intimate encounter with the Spiritual Exercises throughout their lives. Because of this, again and again, we experience this great, wonderful, jubilant experience of God's mercy. When we think of ourselves as sinners, therefore, it actually brings us a humble, sober joy. Yes, a joy to think of ourselves as sinners! It brings us joy, not because of anything we've done, but because of what God has done. That sinful place in me is that intimate place where the Lord has done his most mighty work, where the Lord has been most loving towards me. And for that reason, I rejoice. We are so happy and joyful that the Lord has forgiven us of our sins that every time we think about those sins, instead of guilt we feel this wonderful joy—the joy of knowing that the Lord has forgiven us.

The psalmist says, "My sin is always before me" (Psalm 51:5). I love that line. For many people, that may sound a bit morbid and depressing, but for me it brings me joy because it reminds me that the Lord has forgiven me every minute that I walk on the face of the earth. I am walking around as a redeemed sinner, and this brings me joy.

The Church has a long tradition of thinking of sin in this strangely joyful way, though we don't often look at it very closely. For example, St. Francis de Sales speaks of our sins as our "dear imperfections."[2] He says that on the one hand, God hates our faults because they are faults; but on the other hand, in a certain sense, God loves our faults since they give him an opportunity to show his mercy. They also give us an opportunity to remain humble and to understand and sympathize with the faults of our neighbors.

A similar sentiment is sung about in the beautiful ancient hymn called the *Exsultet*. The deacon sings the *Exsultet* each year in the Easter Vigil service as we emerge from physical darkness and light the Paschal candle. The middle of the song contains these amazing words:

to ransom a slave you gave away your Son!
O truly necessary sin of Adam, . . .
O happy fault
that earned so great, so glorious a Redeemer![3]

With great joy, the deacon sings about our "necessary sin." What does this mean?

Julian of Norwich says our sin was "necessary" because it's the very place where we encountered the unbelievable love that God has for us. It's the place of our salvation.[4] Robert Llewelyn, a wonderful spiritual writer, helps us understand this further in his commentary on the writings of Julian of Norwich. Llewelyn says that when he thinks about his own sins, he can see them as necessary because they represent the place where he has encountered Christ. But what about those whom we have hurt by our sins, he asks. Could they think the same thing about sin being necessary? Llewelyn answers, "I can only hope."[5] We can have faith that God will make good of those wounds that were caused by our sins. We can only hope and pray that God will bring others to a greater healing through the wounds caused by our sinfulness. We can only hope that this experience of our sinning against them will allow them to become an instrument of our own redemption, and that is the greatest call any human being can have. And so, indeed, we have joy in our hearts because of our sins—not because we like our sins, but because the Lord has forgiven us.

Finally, what does it do for us if we keep these truths close to our hearts? What sort of person does this make us out to be, if we have joy upon remembering our sins because of the victorious mercy of God? To answer this, I'd like to give an example from my own life.

Years ago, when I was a young Jesuit, I wanted to take a trip across the country for a particular reason, and it was for a reason that most of the time, our Jesuit superiors don't allow us to take trips. Nonetheless, I went to the superior and asked him to make an exception for this trip. He asked about the details, and though I never exactly lied, neither did I really tell him all of the facts. Had I told him all of the facts, he probably would have said no. Yet because I kept some of the facts from him, he let me go on this trip. I took the trip and have regretted it ever since because I know that I was disobedient. In that moment, I did not live up to the ideals of my vows.

So this is my sin that is "always before me" (Psalm 51:5). I do know I'm forgiven for it, but still it's before me always, and here's how it has come to good use. Years later, I became a novice director. One day, one of my novices was to take a trip. He could have taken a bus or a plane, but it wasn't a very long trip, so I asked him to take a bus. Later, he came back into the office to explain to me why he should be taking a plane. Later still, before making my decision about whether he would travel by bus or by plane, I found out that he had not told me all of the details. And some of the details that he left out would have seriously influenced my decision. So I called him in.

How do you think I acted in front of this novice, knowing that my own sin is before me always? I myself, years before, had tripped into the same pothole on the road to Christ! So I wasn't cruel toward the novice, nor was I judgmental or harsh. Instead, with great tenderness and with great joy, I communicated something to the effect of, "Come on in; let's get you forgiven. I know what it's like to fall into that pit. I fell in that same pit myself years ago."

So come on in, fellow sinners, and let's get ourselves forgiven! This is what it's like to know yourself to be a sinner loved and redeemed by God. This is what it's like to have the joy in your heart of knowing that you sinned and that God has forgiven you. It leads you to be an incredibly kind, gentle, and compassionate person.

Today, I challenge you to celebrate your sins. Celebrate your sins because God has forgiven you of them. God has healed you from them, even making them an instrument of salvation for you—perhaps even, we can hope, for the people that you've hurt.

Let us close once again with our Scripture passage for today.

Closing Prayer

But now we must celebrate and rejoice, because our brother was dead and has come to life again; he was lost and has been found. (Luke 15:32)

Amen.

Day 8

The Second Week

Bible Passage: Matthew 9:35-36

Welcome to Day 8 of *Ascending with Ignatius*. Congratulations! You've made it through the First Week of the Spiritual Exercises. We now begin the Second Week, where we reflect on two things. First, we reflect on Jesus Christ's life from the Incarnation up to, but not including, his passion and death. Second, we look at the question of discipleship: What does it mean to be a disciple of Jesus Christ?

Our first reflection, on this first day of the Second Week, is on the Incarnation. Before we start to look at the life of Christ, we want to ask ourselves these questions: Why did Christ come? Why did the Incarnation happen in the first place?

Let us begin, as we always do, with a prayer based on our Scripture verse for the day.

Opening Prayer

In the name of the Father and of the Son and of the Holy Spirit.

Jesus went around to all the towns and villages, teaching in their synagogues, proclaiming the gospel of the kingdom, and curing every disease and illness. At the sight of the crowds, his heart was moved with pity for them because they were troubled and abandoned, like sheep without a shepherd. (Matthew 9:35-36)

Amen.

Reflection

St. Ignatius would have us begin the Second Week by looking upon the Trinity, whose gaze is upon us. Ignatius asks us to reflect on the moment when the Trinity decided for Jesus the Son to become a member of the human race. He has us imagine all the people on the face of the earth: the people working, the people sleeping, all the people of all different races. Some are tall, he says, and some are short. Some are doing good, and some are doing evil. Then, he says, look at the Trinity gazing upon all these people and listen in. Listen in to what the Trinity is saying within itself.

The Trinity looks upon the earth, says Ignatius, and this is what the Trinity says: "We must go to them; we must work redemption on the world." Remember that Ignatius was around in the sixteenth century, a time when many in the Church saw God as an angry god who did not think highly of humans because of their sinfulness. Ignatius paints this very merciful, kind, and gentle image of the Trinity looking upon the earth, seeing all the bad we're doing, and saying, "We must go and work redemption." It's a beautiful image. And it's an incredibly unbelievable response of our Creator God. Why would our Creator God want to work redemption within us unless he saw us as lovable and redeemable?

When I was a little kid, we sometimes went to the beach for our vacations. At Galveston Beach in Texas, we would float around in the water and play in the sand. We didn't buy those floaty beach toys you find in a store; my dad was a farmer, so he would inflate inner tubes from tractor wheels for us to play with and float on in the water. The inner tubes from the huge rear wheels on the tractor could hold three or four people, but the ones from the smaller front wheels were perfect for one small kid. I was the youngest, and I loved having my very own little inner tube to float in.

With the waves splashing and throwing me around, my dad held on to my inner tube. He didn't want to let it go because he knew that I wasn't able to handle myself very well in the water. Of course, I didn't like my dad holding my inner tube.

I wanted to be on my own, and I kept trying to tear away from him. I didn't typically succeed, but at one point I finally did tear away from my dad, probably just a few feet from him. Just then, a big wave came and tossed me around and turned me upside down. My little legs sticking straight up in the air, this inner tube that once held me safe above water was now trapping my head beneath the surface. All I could see was water everywhere, as it rushed into my mouth and choked me. It was a terrifying moment that seemed like an eternity but in reality was probably just a few seconds. My dad immediately came and flipped me right back over, and everything was fine. I coughed and choked a little bit, my brothers probably laughed at me, and then we just moved on.

When I think about Ignatius' image of the Trinity looking down on the earth seeing us lost, I imagine my dad. I picture my dad looking at me with my little feet sticking up in the air, desperate and unable to save myself. I picture the Trinity making the same conclusion that my dad did: "We must go to him. We must go and redeem. We must go and save."

In our Scripture reading today, Jesus looks upon the crowd and is "moved with pity for them" because they are "like sheep without a shepherd" (Matthew 9:36). He looks upon them with great tenderness and pity. I think this notion first came to Christ within the Trinity when they were looking upon the face of the earth. They saw the people of the earth, and they said, "They are like sheep without a shepherd; they are lost. Let us go to them. We must go to them." They reacted the same way a loving father reacts to his son who is drowning: "We must go to them!"

I don't know a whole lot about sheep, but I'm fairly certain that, without a shepherd, a flock of sheep in first-century Palestine would not have lasted long. Very quickly, they would have been devoured by wild beasts. Shepherdless sheep have no hope and no direction. They're in grave danger. So Jesus saying that they are like sheep without a shepherd is precisely what I think the Trinity must have thought and felt in making the choice for the Incarnation.

I ask you to reflect on that on the passage today. Think about the Trinity looking down upon the earth with great tenderness and making the most loving, self-sacrificial decision that they could have made—"We must go to them! We must save them!" Rejoice at this wonderful God who chooses to come himself and save us.

We close with the Scripture passage once again.

Closing Prayer

Jesus went around to all the towns and villages, teaching in their synagogues, proclaiming the gospel of the kingdom, and curing every disease and illness. At the sight of the crowds, his heart was moved with pity for them because they were troubled and abandoned, like sheep without a shepherd. (Matthew 9:35-36)

Amen.

Day 9

The Second Week

Bible Passage: Luke 1:26-38

Welcome to Day 9. We are at the beginning of the Second Week, wherein we reflect on the life of Christ and on our lives as disciples of Christ. Today we reflect on the story of the Annunciation: when the angel Gabriel visits Mary to announce God's plan for her to give birth to Jesus.

For our opening prayer, we will read snippets from that story, which is found in Luke 1:26-38.

Opening Prayer

In the name of the Father and of the Son and of the Holy Spirit.

In the sixth month, the angel Gabriel was sent from God to a town of Galilee called Nazareth, to a virgin betrothed to a man named Joseph.... And coming to her, he said, "Hail, favored one! The Lord is with you."... Then the angel said to her, "Do not be afraid, Mary, for you have found favor with God. Behold, you will conceive in your womb and bear a son, and you shall name him Jesus."... Mary said, "Behold, I am the handmaid of the Lord. May it be done to me according to your word." Then the angel departed from her. (Luke 1:26-27, 28, 30-31, 38)

Amen.

Reflection

When I was a novice at the age of eighteen, I went through my own thirty-day retreat. It was not an at-home retreat, like this one, but a full thirty days of silence and prayer. One of my favorite moments of the retreat was when we reflected on the Annunciation. I remember looking at this beautiful oak tree from the second-floor balcony of our retreat house in Louisiana, and I saw in my prayerful imagination the angel Gabriel coming to visit Mary. Mary was exactly my age, in my imagination—eighteen years old. The angel said to Mary, "Will you go? Will you go and bear Jesus for the world?" Mary said, "Yes, I will go," and she went.

And then everything changed in my prayer and in my imagination. I saw the angel Gabriel coming to visit me and asking, "Mark, will you go? Will you go and bear Jesus for the world?" And I said, "Yes," and I went. It was a beautiful prayer time that I still remember to this day.

Decades later, I went on an eight-day retreat, and I wanted to repeat that same prayer time because I had gotten so much out of it the first time. So in my retreat house, I set out my Bible beside my chair, opened to the Lucan passage, and made a strong cup of coffee early in the morning before sunrise. (I even opened the window so that Gabriel could get through easier!) I sat in my prayer chair and read that passage of the Annunciation and waited for Gabriel and Mary to show up. I waited and waited and waited, but no one showed up.

After a good while, Mary finally came by, but she wasn't eighteen anymore. Mary was my age—in her forties now. I told Mary I wanted to have that prayer time again, when the angel visited her and told her to go and she went. And Mary said to me, wistfully, "Oh yes, I remember that well, but you know Mark, that was a lot of loads of laundry ago." What? A lot of loads of laundry ago? What was Mary was trying to tell me?

In prayer, I came to understand her message. Those moments of *go* are the sort of romantic moments in our vocation story. They are the moments when we get this clear sense of a call and we say yes to the angel whispering "Go" in our ear. But Mary says that after that "go," there are a lot of loads of laundry. She said to me that day, "Do you notice the last line of that Lucan story?" I grabbed my Bible and read down to the last line: "Then the angel departed from her." Mary was saying to me that after that moment of *go*, there are days and days, weeks and weeks, years and decades of *stays*. She said, "You know down on earth, you all are all excited about the moment of *go*, the moment of your vocation when you say yes, but really, discipleship has much more to do with *stay* than with *go*."

Indeed, most of discipleship is *stay*. It's staying with the commitment that we made when we said that we would go. And that *stay* is sometimes difficult because it may require that we do the same thing every day, day in and day out, over and over again.

Just before Jesus died, he gave what we call the farewell discourses in John's Gospel. Some of his very last words to the disciples were "Remain in my love" (15:9). The reason he's telling the disciples to remain on their very last days together is because he knew that this might be the most difficult part. As difficult as it is at times for us to say yes when the angel tells us to go, it is perhaps even more difficult to stay day after day after day, after the years and years have gone by.

I had the privilege of living with a lot of our retired Jesuit priests and brothers for a while, a number of whom had dementia. As the years went on, they were losing their memory and their cognition. They couldn't remember their own story, they couldn't remember their parents, and sometimes they couldn't remember that they were priests or Jesuits. Some couldn't remember even their own name. But as they sat at Mass and the priest behind the altar began to pray the Eucharistic prayer, they all chimed in. They all prayed the Eucharistic prayer together with the presider. If I was the presider, I would often speak quietly so that I could prayerfully listen to them saying those sacred words. And I realized that the very last language of a priest with dementia is the language of the Eucharist, the language of the Mass, because they've been saying it every day all their lives. I want to be that kind of priest. I want to stay like those elderly priests. I want to stay like Mary. I want to go when Gabriel calls me to go, but I want to stay after Gabriel leaves.

I encourage you today to read the story of Gabriel's visit to Mary. Read when Mary said yes to the angel's call to go, but then think about Mary's story after that. Think about how Mary had to stay behind and raise a child and serve the family as every mom and dad do. Think about your own story. Is there a time when the angel came to visit you? In other words, is there a time when you felt a true calling? It may have been a calling to be a mom, a calling to be a teacher, or any other calling. Then think about how many days of "stay" you were called to, all the way to the present moment, after that initial commitment of "go." Pray to the Lord that you might be that sort of faithful disciple like those elderly priests with dementia. Ask for the grace to be like the first disciple, Mary, who went when she was told to go but also who stayed every day after that.

Let us close, as we always do, with our Scripture passage.

Closing Prayer

In the sixth month, the angel Gabriel was sent from God to a town of Galilee called Nazareth, to a virgin betrothed to a man named Joseph. . . . And coming to her, he said, "Hail, favored one! The Lord is with you." . . . Then the angel said to her, "Do not be afraid, Mary, for you have found favor with God. Behold, you will conceive in your womb and bear a son, and you shall name him Jesus." . . . Mary said, "Behold, I am the handmaid of the Lord. May it be done to me according to your word." Then the angel departed from her. (Luke 1:26-27, 28, 30-31, 38)

Amen.

Day 10

The Second Week

Bible Passage: Luke 2:1-14

Merry Christmas! Today we will be reflecting on the Nativity of Christ. We are early in the Second Week of the Spiritual Exercises, and today we will be pondering the wonderful mystery of Jesus' birth.

Let us begin with today's Scripture passage. I recommend you pray over Luke 2:1-14.

Opening Prayer

In the name of the Father and of the Son and of the Holy Spirit.

While they were [in Bethlehem], the time came for [Mary] to have her child, and she gave birth to her firstborn son.

She wrapped him in swaddling clothes and laid him in a manger, because there was no room for them in the inn. (Luke 2:6-7)

Amen.

Reflection

Today I recommend you reflect on the question of what the baby Jesus was. In the eyes of the world, Jesus was a poor baby born to a poor family in a poor village in a poor nation. In the eyes of the world, the baby Jesus was completely insignificant. We see this by the fact that the baby Jesus was born in a manger. Even if you happened to live in the town of Bethlehem, if you did not happen to know the shepherds or run into the Wise Men on their way to the stable, then this baby born in poverty would not have marked anything special for you. This event would not have shown up in your consciousness at all. This baby seemed to be completely and entirely insignificant, and yet we know that this baby turned out to be the Savior of the world.

Today I want to reflect on the question of whether that same pattern of God's action is true for us. Might it be true that God shows up in seemingly insignificant ways again and again? Does God continue to choose to become present in the world in small ways that escape our notice?

Take this very retreat, *Ascending with Ignatius*, as an example. I first gave this retreat on YouTube with the idea of doing something as a pastor for my parishioners during the Covid-19 crisis. I had hoped to get fifty or maybe a hundred of my parishioners to follow along. It was a small and insignificant thing, not meant to become anything of great reach. And yet it turned out to be a worldwide event. Thirty thousand people from all over the world tuned in to the online retreat. The largest crowd that I have ever spoken to in my thirty years as a Jesuit has been one thousand people. That's thirty times larger than the largest audience I've ever addressed! Yet in my mind, this retreat was as small and insignificant as a poor baby born in a poor village some two thousand years ago.

I suspect that this might be true in your own lives as well. Today I challenge you to first read and reflect over the Scripture passage of the Nativity and ask yourself, Has this ever happened in your past? Can you look back over the years and find something that looked small and insignificant to you at the time but turned out to be a manifestation of God's presence in your life? Look back at that moment and marvel at it. Relish it. Relish the "baby Jesus" being born in your own life. Thank God for that moment in the past.

Secondly, ask yourself: Where is that baby Jesus in my life today? What is something or someone who, in your estimation, is small and insignificant but may well be God's choice of manifesting himself to you today in your present state? Might you pray about that today? Maybe you will

find yourself a wiser person for having done this exercise—
someone who has discerned that what seems insignificant
to everyone else has actually turned out to be the very manifestation of God's presence.

Closing Prayer

While they were [in Bethlehem], the time came for [Mary]
to have her child, and she gave birth to her firstborn son. She
wrapped him in swaddling clothes and laid him in a manger,
because there was no room for them in the inn. (Luke 2:6-7)

Amen.

Day 11

The Second Week

Bible Passage: Luke 2:39-40

Welcome to Day 11 of *Ascending with Ignatius*. We are in the Second Week, reflecting on the life of Christ. Having reflected on the Annunciation, when the angel Gabriel visited Mary, and on the Nativity, when the baby Jesus was born, today we will reflect on the hidden life of Christ. As you probably know, there were years and years about which little is written of Jesus. We hear almost nothing about Jesus's youth, adolescence, and young adulthood, all the way up to the age of about thirty. I would like to ask you to reflect on those years. We will ask Jesus himself to reveal some of what happened to him in those hidden years.

Today's verse will be Luke 2:39-40.

Opening Prayer

In the name of the Father and of the Son and of the Holy Spirit.

When they had fulfilled all the prescriptions of the law of the Lord, [the Holy Family] returned to Galilee, to their own town of Nazareth. The child grew and became strong, filled with wisdom; and the favor of God was upon him. (Luke 2:39-40)

Amen.

Reflection

Today, I'm giving you a bit of an unusual challenge. There's a good chance that you've never prayed about what the Church calls the "hidden life" of Jesus. There is this strange gap in the story of Jesus. We have stories of his birth. We have the story of his very young life when Mary and Joseph find him in the Temple. Then the stories stop. It says in Luke's Gospel that he grew in wisdom and strength for years and was obedient to his parents.

Pope Francis has some wonderful things to say about these hidden years. He said,

We are certainly moved by the story of how the adolescent Jesus followed the religious calendar of the community and the social duties; in knowing how, as a young worker, he worked with Joseph; and then how he attended the reading of the Scriptures, in praying the psalms, and in so many other customs of daily life. The Gospels, in their sobriety, make no reference to Jesus' adolescence and leave this task to our loving meditation.

Art, literature, music have taken this journey through imagination.[6]

Pope Francis says that the Gospels leave to our imagination and "our loving meditation" the task of learning about the hidden life of Jesus. So let us take on Pope Francis' challenge. Let us engage our imagination in loving meditation to find out what happened to Jesus in his hidden life. I have done this exercise many times in my prayer life, and it has always proven fruitful.

When you ask Jesus to tell you about his hidden life, he will oblige. The one obstacle will be your own lack of faith, your own doubting. You may think, "If I try to ask the Lord about his hidden life, I might imagine him as, say, a tall adolescent boy who is shy. Well, what if my next-door neighbor prays the same Exercise, and she imagines Jesus to be short and outgoing? Does this mean that one of us has to be wrong?" Well, perhaps in terms of the accuracy of the historical Jesus, I suppose so. Or you might both be wrong, but none of that is really all that important. What I'm suggesting here is that God wants to manifest himself again and again in our world and in our lives, and one way God does this is through your imagination and loving meditation. If you give God a chance, he will once again incarnate himself into the world, but this time in your prayerful imagination. Try to trust it as the message Jesus is trying to tell you in the present tense. Whether or not it is accurate according to the physical characteristics or life events of Jesus two thousand years ago is less important. What is Jesus trying to instruct you about his very self through your imagination and meditation?

Jesus was present two thousand years ago, but Jesus is also present here today. So I encourage you to go to Jesus in your prayer time and to ask him to reveal his hidden life. Go through this imaginative assignment as a sort of playful exercise. What was his adolescence like? Did he struggle like so many adolescents of every age? Did he have a lot of friends or just a few? Was he attracted to anyone or not? Did he have a deep religious sense all the way through, or did he grow in that? Did he ever have struggles with his parents? We know that he never sinned, but it's not necessarily a sin to struggle with your parents, especially during adolescence. Did he have heartbreak? Was he ever rejected by his friends? Did he ever experience failure? If Christ was like us in all things but sin, and it's not necessarily a sin to fail, then perhaps in his adolescence, he experienced some sort of failure.

If you speak with the Lord about this, if you ask the Lord to reveal a part of his hidden life, he will inflame your imagination and teach you something about his very self, regardless of what exactly happened two thousand years ago. He will show you his current self, his present self, and he will teach you something about what it means to follow him as his disciple. Trust in that as you go through the day, and have a little fun with it. This is meant to be a playful prayer day where the Lord reveals a bit of what is usually the most awkward phase of anyone's life. So enjoy your day with the Lord. Let him reminisce awhile with you about his adolescence. Thank the Lord for being your intimate friend.

Let us close with praying with our Scripture passage from Luke once again.

Closing Prayer

When they had fulfilled all the prescriptions of the law of the Lord, [the Holy Family] returned to Galilee, to their own town of Nazareth. The child grew and became strong, filled with wisdom; and the favor of God was upon him. (Luke 2:39-40)

Amen.

Day 12

The Second Week

Bible Passage: Luke 4:1-14

Welcome to Day 12. We are in the Second Week of the Exercises wherein we accompany Jesus through his life. We have been to the Annunciation, where the angel Gabriel announced the birth of Christ to Mary. We have been at that birth in the Nativity, and we have visited Jesus' hidden life and reflected on his adolescence. Today we reflect on the beginning of his public life. Jesus went into the Jordan to be baptized by John, and then he went immediately into the desert to be tempted. The temptation of Jesus is the theme of our reflection today.

Today's Scripture passage is Luke 4:1-14.

Opening Prayer

In the name of the Father and of the Son and of the Holy
Spirit.

Filled with the holy Spirit, Jesus returned from the Jordan
and was led by the Spirit into the desert for forty days, to be
tempted by the devil. He ate nothing during those days, and
when they were over he was hungry. The devil said to him,
"If you are the Son of God, command this stone to become
bread." Jesus answered him, "It is written, 'One does not live
by bread alone.'" Then he took him up and showed him all
the kingdoms of the world in a single instant. The devil said
to him, "I shall give to you all this power and their glory. . . .
All this will be yours, if you worship me." Jesus said to him
in reply, "It is written:

> 'You shall worship the Lord, your God,
>   and him alone shall you serve.'"

Then he led him to Jerusalem, made him stand on the parapet of the temple, and said to him, "If you are the Son of
God, throw yourself down from here, for it is written:

> 'He will command his angels concerning you,
>   to guard you,'

and:

'With their hands they will support you,
   lest you dash your foot against a stone.'"

Jesus said to him in reply, "It also says, 'You shall not put the Lord, your God, to the test.'" . . . Jesus returned to Galilee in the power of the Spirit. (Luke 4:1-6, 7-12, 14)

Amen.

Reflection

Before we look at the temptations of Jesus, I'd like you to think back at the temptation of Adam and Eve in the garden in the third chapter of Genesis. We tend to think of that event as a temptation to eat a piece of fruit, but it can't be just about fruit. The true root of the temptation of Adam and Eve is this: they were tempted to be like God. The snake said to Adam and Eve that if they would eat this fruit, they would be like God in a very particular way. He told Eve that eating the fruit would give them divine knowledge—to know the things that God knows.

This same temptation experienced by Adam and Eve—to become like God—is present in all three temptations of Jesus in the desert. For us too, every time we are tempted to do wrong, it is a temptation to reject our humanity and to try (feebly) to become like God. Let's look now at the temptations of Jesus.

The first temptation of Jesus is to satisfy his hunger. Of course, this means much more than the hunger of the stomach. Humans have so many hungers and thirsts, and we're constantly trying to satisfy them. Many times, rather than embracing our state of being hungry or thirsty, we grasp at things we are not called to grasp at. We try to quench our hunger and thirst. Jesus shows us the way by embracing his hunger, by not running from it. He accepts his hunger as part of his humanity.

Second, Jesus is tempted towards power. The devil says that Jesus can have all the power of the kingdoms of the earth, but Jesus instead embraces the powerlessness of his humanity. We humans frequently feel powerless. Oftentimes, when we look back at the biggest mistakes of our lives, they were probably at moments when we felt somehow powerless, and we were lashing out. We were desperately trying to regain power at a moment when, probably subconsciously, we felt powerless. Jesus embraces powerlessness through his humanity.

Finally, Jesus is tempted towards security. The devil tells Jesus he can throw himself off the Temple because the angels will catch him, lest he dash his foot against the stone. The truth is, you and I are constantly afraid. We're constantly and rightly afraid of being harmed, of dashing our feet against the stone. The truth is, at any moment, harm can come to us. We can be stricken ill; we could have some sort of accident; even death might be right around the corner. Because of this, humans can feel insecure all the time. And sometimes we make our biggest mistakes because of our fears. Our fears lead us to grasp at the divinity that we are not called to. Jesus instead grasps at his humanity, and he calls you and me to do the same.

I hope you now can see more clearly how all the temptations—having divine knowledge, having no hungers or thirst, being powerful, and having complete security—come down to being like God. This ultimate temptation originated with our first parents in the Garden, and from it come all other temptations. And Jesus' answer to this problem is to model for us an embrace of our humanity. Pray today over the temptations of Jesus, and try to be a great disciple by following his lead. Accept and embrace your humanity. Accept and embrace your lack of knowledge, your hungers and thirsts, your powerlessness, and your lack of security. Place all your trust instead in God, who will fulfill all these needs, bring us into heaven, and make us like himself.

Let us pray.

Closing Prayer

Filled with the holy Spirit, Jesus returned from the Jordan and was led by the Spirit into the desert for forty days, to be tempted by the devil. He ate nothing during those days, and when they were over he was hungry. The devil said to him, "If you are the Son of God, command this stone to become bread." Jesus answered him, "It is written, 'One does not live by bread alone.'" Then he took him up and showed him all the kingdoms of the world in a single instant. The devil said to him, "I shall give to you all this power and their glory. . . . All this will be yours, if you worship me." Jesus said to him in reply, "It is written:

'You shall worship the Lord, your God,
　　and him alone shall you serve.'"

Then he led him to Jerusalem, made him stand on the parapet of the temple, and said to him, "If you are the Son of God, throw yourself down from here, for it is written:

'He will command his angels concerning you,
　　to guard you,'

and:

'their hands they will support you,
　　lest you dash your foot against a stone.'"

Jesus said to him in reply, "It also says, 'You shall not put the Lord, your God, to the test.'" . . . Jesus returned to Galilee in the power of the Spirit. (Luke 4:1-6, 7-12, 14)

Amen.

Day 13

The Second Week

Bible Passage: Luke 5:1-11

Welcome to Day 13. We are in the middle of the Second Week of the Spiritual Exercises, where we accompany Christ in his entire life. We've been through the Annunciation, the Nativity, the hidden life of Christ, and the baptism and temptation of Jesus. Today we see the beginnings of his ministerial life as we reflect on the call of St. Peter.

Today's verse is Luke 5:1-11.

Opening Prayer

In the name of the Father and of the Son and of the Holy Spirit.

After he had finished speaking, [Jesus] said to Simon, "Put out into deep water and lower your nets for a catch." Simon said in reply, "Master we have worked hard all night and have caught nothing, but at your command I will lower the nets." When they had done this, they caught a great number of fish and their nets were tearing. They signaled to their partners in the other boat to come to help them. They came and filled both boats so that they were in danger of sinking. When Simon Peter saw this, he fell at the knees of Jesus and said, "Depart from me, Lord, for I am a sinful man." For astonishment at the catch of fish they had made seized him. . . . Jesus said to Simon, "Do not be afraid; from now on you will be catching men." When they brought their boats to the shore, they left everything and followed him. (Luke 5:4-9, 10-11)

Amen.

Reflection

It is not an accident that Peter chose to follow Jesus on the very day that started out as the worst day of his fishing career but ended up as his best. There is good evidence that Peter knew Jesus before this day. Capernaum was a very small town, and it seems as though Jesus had been there for a while. Peter likely already knew Jesus, but it was on this day that Peter chose to leave everything and follow him.

This has an important message embedded in it for you and me. It is when our nets are empty that Christ can do his greatest work for us. It is when we are completely empty, when we are spent, that Christ can fill up our lives and do wonders. It is when we feel like a complete and utter failure that Jesus can lead us to an abundant catch in our own life. Corrie ten Boom once said, "We do not know that Jesus is all we need until Jesus is all we have." For St. Peter on that day, Jesus was all he had. He had no fish. He had no skills. He was having a very bad day in his career. Jesus was all he had, and he learned that day that Jesus was all he needed.

When I first started high school teaching, as a twenty-three-year-old Jesuit only a few years older than my students. And that first year was really rough. I hadn't a clue as to how to discipline those adolescent boys, and there were days when my class descended into mayhem. It was the most traumatic experience of my life up to that time.

I was about five years a Jesuit, and everything had gone successfully for me up to that point. And yet, like St. Peter, I was having the worst time of my career. Feeling like a complete failure that first year, my nets were completely empty. I remember waking up in the middle of the night in April of that first year in a cold sweat, screaming, "I hate them! I hate them! I hate them!" Of course, I didn't hate them, but I was so desperate and so empty that I was grasping at anything I could.

So I turned completely to the Lord because I had no other choice. Jesus was all I had. That's when Jesus came to the rescue. With lots of prayer and with the help of my Jesuit superiors, I had a wonderful second year, and by my third year, I was begging my superiors to give me an unprecedented fourth year. It ended up being one of my favorite careers of my entire life. I loved being a high school teacher, but it all began with empty nets. It all began with finally turning over the nets to Jesus so that he could fill them up with his own grace.

When we have success, when we have lots of things that we can rely on besides Jesus, he is not able to do as much work in our lives. It's only when we are empty that he can do his greatest work.

I challenge you today to reflect on a time in your past when you were empty and when Christ seemed to do his greatest work from it—when Christ seemed to fill your empty nets. When did Jesus rescue you from your metaphorical bad classroom year? Think back on that time in the past, and ask yourself how this also might be happening here in the present. The very areas of our lives that we feel are empty—the low points in our lives right now—perhaps, if we rely on the Lord, we will find them full of his grace after he has finished speaking.

Let us close by prayerfully reading our Scripture passage once more.

Closing Prayer

After he had finished speaking, [Jesus] said to Simon, "Put out into deep water and lower your nets for a catch." Simon said in reply, "Master we have worked hard all night and have caught nothing, but at your command I will lower the nets." When they had done this, they caught a great number of fish and their nets were tearing. They signaled to their partners in the other boat to come to help them. They came and filled both boats so that they were in danger of sinking. When Simon Peter saw this, he fell at the knees of Jesus and said, "Depart from me, Lord, for I am a sinful man." For astonishment at the catch of fish they had made seized him. . . . Jesus said to Simon, "Do not be afraid; from now on you will be catching men." When they brought their boats to the shore, they left everything and followed him. (Luke 5:4-9, 10-11)

Amen.

Day 14

The Second Week

Bible Passage: Matthew 5:13-16

Welcome to Day 14 of *Ascending with Ignatius*. We are in the middle of the Second Week of the Spiritual Exercises, wherein we reflect on the life of Christ and the question of discipleship. In the first half of the Second Week, we reflected on the earlier scenes from Christ's life. Now in the second half, we look at his public ministry, leading us to the question of discipleship at the end of the Second Week. After having reflected on the life and words of Jesus, we will ask ourselves, What does this tell us about discipleship? What does it mean to be a disciple today?

Today, we reflect on Matthew 5:13-16.

Opening Prayer

In the name of the Father and of the Son and of the Holy Spirit.

You are the salt of the earth. But if salt loses its taste, with what can it be seasoned? It is no longer good for anything but to be thrown out and trampled underfoot. You are the light of the world. A city set on a mountain cannot be hidden. Nor do they light a lamp and then put it under a bushel basket; it is set on a lampstand, where it gives light to all in the house. Just so, your light must shine before others, that they may see your good deeds and glorify your heavenly Father. (Matthew 5:13-16)

Amen.

Reflection

Being called salty doesn't seem like a compliment. Imagine that your beloved tells you that you are like a beautiful painting in a museum, and you reply, "Well, honey, I think you are like table salt." It doesn't sound like a great compliment, but we have to remember that in first-century Palestine, they had practically no access to seasoning, including salt, for most of their lives. Only a few times in their lives, for special occasions like weddings or other big ceremonies, would they have seasoning on their food. Imagine if you lived your whole life eating terribly bland food, and then one day you got to eat a wonderful meal that had just the right amount of salt. Wouldn't you think wonderfully about salt? So when Jesus says, "You are the salt of the earth" (Matthew 5:13), they remember those wonderful occasions like their own wedding, when they had the rare privilege of tasting salt. It's a great compliment in their book.

About thirty years ago, when I was a young seminarian, this kind woman made a cake for the seminarians to share. The only problem was that she forgot to put any sugar in it! Not even a grain. It tasted so awful we couldn't eat it. Food that has no seasoning can be so bland as to become inedible. When Jesus is telling us that we are the salt of the earth, especially as disciples, he's saying that we disciples are called to season the world. We're called to flavor the world. Most of the world, as you know, is quite secular. Many people hardly ever pray in church. It is we who go to church regularly and who pray regularly who are called to season the world with the faith, hope, and love of Jesus.

Seasoning the world requires responsibility. It may not be easy because we have to discern how to do it. I once had the opposite experience of my cake story from thirty years ago. I was helping a brother Jesuit from a different country who had no experience cooking. He was cooking our supper for the community that night, and I gave him a recipe for chicken with a wonderful sauce. While he was cooking, he ran into my room and said, "You have to come help; it tastes terrible!"

I went into the kitchen and tasted it, and, sure enough, it was just awful. So I said, "Let's go through each item on the recipe then. "You put this in, right?" "You put that in, right?" Then I said, "Did you put in the two teaspoons of salt?" And he held up a cup and said, "Yes, I put two of these in the sauce." He had put two cups of salt in this sauce! This funny little story relates to our vocation of seasoning the world. The world becomes bland without the faith, hope, and love of Jesus with which we season it, but what if we come on too strong? What if we are so aggressive with our faith life that we shove and push faith on other people? Might this be like using two cups of salt in a dish? Might it be so strong for people who aren't used to it that they will just turn away?

Finally, salt does not draw attention to itself. Imagine you go to a friend's house, and there's a wonderful chicken dinner there. You and your spouse are driving home again, and you say, "Boy, wasn't that a wonderful dish of salt with a bit of chicken in it? Wasn't that salt just delicious?" You would never say that, would you? No, you would talk about how wonderful the chicken dish was, and you wouldn't even mention the salt at all. So when Jesus tells us that we are salt of the earth, he's trying to make a subtle message here.

As salt, we are called to bring out the flavors of the world, which are ultimately God's flavors of faith, hope, and love. We don't bring our own flavors; we enhance the flavors that are already there. That's our calling, and we know we are doing it right when no one is paying attention to us but paying attention rather to God, paying attention to God's faith, hope, and love.

The end of this Gospel story says that you will do good works, and people will give glory to God. He didn't say that people will give glory to us because of our good works but that our good works will lead people to give glory to God. You will be like salt; you will bring out the flavors of faith, hope, and love that already exist in the world.

Let us close, once again, with our passage from Scripture.

Closing Prayer

You are the salt of the earth. But if salt loses its taste, with what can it be seasoned? It is no longer good for anything but to be thrown out and trampled underfoot. You are the light of the world. A city set on a mountain cannot be hidden. Nor do they light a lamp and then put it under a bushel basket; it is set on a lampstand where it gives light to all in the house. Just so, your light must shine before others, so that they may see your good deeds and glorify your heavenly Father. (Matthew 5:13-16)

Amen.

Day 15

The Second Week

Bible Passages: Mark 7:31-37; John 2:1-12; Luke 19:1-10

Welcome to Day 15. Today we will do something a little different. I'm giving you three Scripture passages instead of just one. And they are from three different Gospel writers: Mark, Luke, and John. I invite you to read these passages well and try to get a sense not only of what Jesus is doing but the way Jesus is doing it. What is going on inside of Jesus? What seems to be his agenda? What is his purpose in performing these particular miracles with these particular people?

Let us begin by praying over part of the passage from Mark.

Opening Prayer

In the name of the Father and of the Son and of the Holy Spirit.

And people brought to [Jesus] a deaf man who had a speech impediment and begged him to lay his hand on him. He took him off by himself away from the crowd. He put his finger into the man's ears and, spitting, touched his tongue; then he looked up to heaven and groaned, and said to him, "*Ephphatha*!" (that is, "Be opened!") And [immediately] the man's ears were opened, his speech impediment was removed, and he spoke plainly. (Mark 7:32-35)

Amen.

Reflection

In the Second Week, St. Ignatius asks that we gaze lovingly on our Lord, that we look long at what Jesus is doing. We try to see not only the actual concrete behaviors but try to get a sense of what Jesus is up to. What is his agenda as he's performing these various miracles? This will give us the insight that we need as we try to live as disciples of Christ. So let us look a little deeper at this story.

The people brought this man to Jesus demanding his healing. What was the crowd's agenda? Maybe they wanted to see a magic trick. As Jesus went from town to town, some of the Pharisees wanted him to perform miracles to trap him somehow, by breaking a law, but others were just curious and wanted to see a magic trick. Is that what was going on with this crowd? They seemed to be almost shoving this man in front of Jesus. Imagine yourself a first-century Palestinian person who cannot hear or speak, you're stuck in the middle of this fracas, and you're shoved before a stranger. It must have been very disorienting for the man, even traumatic. He must have been terribly confused, not understanding why they were pushing and shoving him.

Jesus could have healed this man instantly, dazzling the crowd, but that's not what he did. Instead, he took the man off by himself, away from the spotlight. He wanted the man to be relieved of the frightening chaos that was all around him. Then, silently gesturing to the man's ears and tongue, Jesus quietly communicated with him in a way that showed that he understood this man's world. Jesus, unlike the crowd, took the time to tend to this man's personal needs. He found a way not just to heal him but to connect with him. This was the beginning of the miracle: that finally someone stopped and made an effort to communicate with this man who had a hard time hearing and a hard time speaking.

Let's go to a second story and see if we see a common factor here. The second story is the miracle of Jesus producing wine from water at the wedding banquet in John 2. This couple is so happy that they have gotten married; they've invited all their friends and family. And they run out of wine.

How do you think the couple must have felt as the wine was running out? How would you have felt if you had a party and the food and drinks start to run out? And so Mary and Jesus scheme together. Mary says to Jesus, "They've run out of wine," and Jesus *publicly* says, "Oh that's not anything to do with me, you know." But then Mary and Jesus seemed to work behind the scenes.

Mary tells the servants to do whatever Jesus tells them, and Jesus tells them to fill those jars with water and take a little water to the chef. Tasting the wine, the chef doesn't know anything that's happened, only that someone has now brought out the best wine. Jesus has done this work so quietly that the head chef hasn't even noticed what's going on with his own servants! The bride and groom don't notice, nor do the guests. Jesus performs this entire miracle without anybody noticing. He does it in this quiet way, such that only Mary and the disciples really know what happened. It seems, more than any concern, that Jesus was interested in saving the couple embarrassment and dishonor. He wanted the positive attention to be always on the couple and their joyous day instead of on himself as some sort of miracle-working superstar. Perhaps that's what Jesus meant when he said to Mary, "My time is not yet here" (John 7:6). Rather than turning this moment into his hour, Jesus saved the day for the couple. And no one knew what a wonderful thing Jesus had done for them.

When you put this together with the story of the deaf and mute man, do you get a picture of the kind of person Jesus was? We see not just that he performed miracles but that he had this tender, special care for each individual, meeting their own personal needs in the moment.

Finally, let's look at the story of Zacchaeus from Luke 19. It tells us that Zacchaeus is a tax collector, which is to say he is one of the most despised people in town. This hated man is also embarrassingly short. Perhaps people made fun of him or jeered at him as he climbed up the sycamore tree to see Jesus. He's at the height of mockery at this point, whereas everyone in the crowd is impressed with Jesus, the superstar of the day. And what does Jesus do? He looks at Zacchaeus up in a tree while everyone is laughing at him and says, "I want to have supper with you." He tells the man he wants to dine with him, to socialize with him!

Again, we see Jesus caring for the tender heart of the person. He's probably the first person in the town to sit and have a meal with Zacchaeus. Companionship is what brought Zacchaeus to Christ. Befriending him—not preaching, scolding, or condemning—is what led him to live a better life.

Looking at these three miracle stories all together, we see not only that Jesus is a miracle worker but that he cares for the body, mind, and soul of the person. He cares for the tender heart of each person he encounters. If Jesus were interested in his own reputation, he would have acted loudly at Cana and secretly at Jericho. But instead, he does the opposite. He not only helps people through a miracle, but he also restores their place in the community. As disciples, you and I are called to do the same. We're called to do everything we can to help people with their hunger and ills, but we're also called to pay attention to their hearts. As Jesus did, we're called to find a way of communicating to the heart of each person, to have a meal with them, to save them from embarrassment. This is the kind of disciple that Christ wishes us to be.

Let us close with one more prayerful reading of our passage.

Closing Prayer

And people brought to [Jesus] a deaf man who had a speech impediment and begged him to lay his hand on him. He took him off by himself away from the crowd. He put his finger into the man's ears and, spitting, touched his tongue; then he looked up to heaven and groaned, and said to him, "*Ephphatha!*" (that is, "Be opened!") And [immediately] the man's ears were opened, his speech impediment was removed, and he spoke plainly. (Mark 7:72-35)

Amen.

Day 16

The Second Week

Bible Passage: John 6:1-13

Welcome to Day 16 of *Ascending with Ignatius*. We are still in the Second Week of the Spiritual Exercises, whereby we explore the question of discipleship as we look at the life of Christ.

Today, we look at Jesus' miracle of multiplying the loaves. This story was a very important one for the early Christians. It seems as though there were at least two incidents of Jesus doing this miracle, and a story of Jesus multiplying food is told six times in the four Gospels. An ancient image of the multiplication of the loaves is one of the Holy Land's most sacred treasures.

Let us begin by using John's telling of the story as our opening prayer.

Opening Prayer

In the name of the Father and of the Son and of the Holy Spirit.

Jesus went across the Sea of Galilee [of Tiberias]. A large crowd followed him, because they saw the signs he was performing on the sick. Jesus went up on the mountain, and there he sat down with his disciples. . . . When Jesus raised his eyes and saw that a large crowd was coming to him, he said to Philip, "Where can we buy enough food for them to eat?" . . . Philip answered him, "Two hundred days' wages worth of food would not be enough for each of them to have a little [bit]." One of his disciples, Andrew, the brother of Simon Peter, said to him, "There is a boy here who has five barley loaves and two fish; but what good are these for so many?" Jesus said, "Have the people recline." Now there was a great deal of grass in that place. So the men reclined, about five thousand in number. Then Jesus took the loaves, gave thanks, and distributed them to those who were reclining, and also as much of the fish as they wanted. When they had had their fill, he said to his disciples, "Gather the fragments left over, so that nothing will be wasted." So they collected them, and filled twelve wicker baskets with fragments from the five barley loaves that had been more than they could eat. (John 6:1-3, 5, 7-13)

Amen.

Reflection

Did Jesus really need the help of the disciples and the boy in the story? In one of the other scriptural stories of the multiplication, Jesus explicitly says to the disciples, "Give them some food yourselves" (Matthew 14:16). This seems to be a strange statement since Jesus was the miracle worker. I chose this particular version from John 6 because I love this image of a small boy giving up his loaves and fishes to help Jesus. Did Jesus need the boy's help? Did he need the help of the other disciples? Clearly he didn't. He could have handled this whole situation all by himself. So, Jesus must be trying to tell us something about discipleship here—about what it means to serve God's people.

Jesus must be trying to tell us that we must all work together to make a miracle. We must feed God's people working cooperatively with one another, even if one disciple can do it all by himself or herself. We should instead be working together as a team, as a community.

Another story in John's Gospel seems to make a similar point. After the resurrection of Jesus, Peter and some of the other disciples are out fishing, but they haven't caught anything all night. Jesus appears on the shore and leads them to an abundant catch just as they are about to call it quits. The story says that Jesus already has breakfast prepared; he's got fish grilling on a campfire on the seashore, and yet as the disciples haul their big catch, he tells the disciples to bring some of their fish to add to his (see John 21:1-14). Surely Jesus could have grilled the right quantity himself. His needing the disciples to add his meal is an indication of Jesus saying, once again, that we work cooperatively with Jesus to make miracles happen. Jesus wants us to work cooperatively with one another as well.

This is an important point for us to keep in mind because Christian leaders often make the big mistake of trying to do everything themselves. *I want to help the people of God,* they think. *I have a strong work ethic, and I'm excited about doing God's work, so I turn down any offers for help from anyone else. I just do it myself.* This is a common mistake among Christian disciples, and Jesus is telling us that we should all be working cooperatively. When we try to do everything ourselves, we potentially create at least three problems in the process.

First, our pride could be getting in the way. We may have a certain pride in wanting to do it ourselves instead of having the courage and the strength to ask for help. This can lead to burnout.

Second, we deprive other disciples of the opportunity to share in the mission. Others may want to serve people as well, and we deprive them of that opportunity.

Third, Jesus himself seems to indicate that somehow the quality of the miracle is higher if we can work together in it. I can name several times in my own ministry when I was setting out to do something all on my own, and then other people pitched in and helped, making the quality of the ministry or service much greater.

So when we read this story of Jesus multiplying the loaves, let us be joyful about his wonderful gift of abundance; and let us trust that Jesus turns to us as his current disciples, saying, "Give them some food yourselves." But let us imagine that Jesus says this to us with the plural "you." Jesus wants us to work together. He wants to allow the small boy in our church to help out with the mission today. Let us dedicate ourselves to be a part of the miracle—to working together to make miracles happen in our Church and in our world.

We close with the same beautiful Gospel passage once more.

Closing Prayer

Jesus went across the Sea of Galilee [of Tiberias]. A large crowd followed him, because they saw the signs he was performing on the sick. Jesus went up on the mountain, and there he sat down with his disciples. . . . When Jesus raised his eyes and saw that a large crowd was coming to him, he said to Philip, "Where can we buy enough food for them to eat?" . . . Philip answered him, "Two hundred days' wages worth of food would not be enough for each of them to have a little [bit]." One of his disciples, Andrew, the brother of Simon Peter, said to him, "There is a boy here who has five barley loaves and two fish; but what good are these for so many?" Jesus said, "Have the people recline." Now there was a great deal of grass in that place. So the men reclined, about five thousand in number. Then Jesus took the loaves, gave thanks, and distributed them to those who were reclining, and also as much of the fish as they wanted. When they had had their fill, he said to his disciples, "Gather the fragments left over, so that nothing will be wasted." So they collected them, and filled twelve wicker baskets with fragments from the five barley loaves that had been more than they could eat. (John 6:1-3, 5, 7-13)

Amen.

Day 17

The Second Week

Bible Passages: Mark 10:17-31; Philippians 1:20-26

Welcome to Day 17 of *Ascending with Ignatius*. We are nearing the end of the Second Week of the Spiritual Exercises. Today we will look at the topic of discipleship in an intense way. I would like to ask you to reflect on two Scripture passages today: Mark 10:17-31 and Philippians 1:20-26. We'll use an excerpt from the Marcan passage as our opening prayer, and turn to St. Paul's words to the Philippians for our closing prayer.

Opening Prayer

In the name of the Father and of the Son and of the Holy Spirit.

As [Jesus] was setting out on a journey, a man ran up, knelt down before him, and asked him, "Good teacher, what must I do to inherit eternal life?" Jesus answered him, . . . "You know the commandments: 'You shall not kill; you shall not commit adultery; you shall not steal; you shall not bear false witness; you shall not defraud; honor your father and your mother.'" He replied and said to him, "Teacher, all of these I have observed from my youth." Jesus, looking at him, loved him and said to him, "You are lacking in one thing. Go, sell what you have, and give to [the] poor and you will have treasure in heaven; then come, follow me." At that statement his face fell, and he went away sad, for he had many possessions. (Mark 10:17-18, 19-22)

Amen.

Reflection

When I was a little kid, I had a yellow lollipop, and I thought to myself, *Maybe God would like me to give him this yellow lollipop.* So I said a little prayer to God; it's the earliest prayer that I can remember saying in my whole life. I held up the lollipop to the heavens and I said, "God, if you wish, you can have this lollipop; I'm ready to give it to you." And I waited just a second. He didn't seem to want it, so I ate it myself!

Ignatius has a wonderful parable called "the three classes of men," which we sometimes call "the three kind of people."

Imagine that these three people all have come into a large sum of money through a business transaction, and all three want to be good disciples of Christ. So they all want to give the money to Christ in some way or another.

The first kind of person talks about it, talks about it, and talks about it some more, but he never gets around to giving away any of the money. This is an all-talk-and-no-action kind of person.

The second person actually does something about it. He decides to give a good chunk of the money away. We can imagine that maybe he gave a large portion of the money to the poor, and he's quite proud of himself for doing that. Ignatius says that while this is a good Christian, he seems to lack one thing. Rather than asking God to show him God's will for how to use the money, he simply decides for himself how much he should give away and to whom.

An example of this in our own age might be the following: Let's say a young woman decides to become a doctor. She goes to medical school, becomes a doctor, and then—in order to serve God—goes off to a third-world country to serve as a missionary doctor. Imagine that later in life, she finds herself quite miserable and starts to pray about it. She begins to realize that God had never asked her to become a doctor; that was simply her own notion. She had decided for herself the way that she would be a disciple rather than asking Christ what she should do with her life. Ignatius says that this second kind of person is a good person but isn't the ideal disciple because these people decide for themselves how to follow Christ rather than asking for God's will.

The third type of person is not what we might expect by this point in the story. First, we have someone who talks about giving the money away but never does. Second, we have someone who gives away a large portion of it. You might think the third person will give it all away, but Ignatius has a wonderful twist in the story. He says that the third person doesn't know what God's will is yet, and so he just holds onto it for a while longer. Then he ends the story there. It ends with a cliff-hanger! You never find out what, if anything, this third person gives.

Ignatius calls the third type of person the ideal disciple. Why? Because this one puts it all at the feet of God. He wants God to decide what to do with it. This third person is ready to give it all away or to keep every single penny of it if that is what God wants him to do. He isn't presumptuous with it, and he doesn't presume that God wants him to give it away. It may be that at the end of their lives, the second person gave away more money to the poor than the third. But the third person is the one who waited on God's will. He decided based on what God wanted rather than what he himself thought would be a good image of discipleship.

You and I are called to give away everything, but only in the sense of handing it over to God and letting God tell us what we should keep and what we should give away. The same goes for discerning when we should act and when we should wait. It is a difficult thing to give away your possessions. It's even more difficult to hold the lollipop. What do I mean? As a little kid, I could have given the lollipop to God. I could also have eaten it (which I did). But the one thing I couldn't do as a kid was hold the lollipop for very long. "Holding the lollipop" is an expression I use for myself when God is asking me to wait. When God has not yet told me what he wants me to do or how he wants me to use my resources for his kingdom, I have to wait. I have to hold a lollipop. In those times, I'm very tempted to decide for myself how to use these resources rather than wait on God. But God is asking me to hold a lollipop.

This takes us to our second passage for today from Paul's Letter to the Philippians. In this first chapter of the letter, St. Paul is saying that he is imprisoned and that he might be executed for being a Christian. Then he says a really interesting thing: he doesn't know whether he wants to live or die. He would die as a martyr, and he thinks that would be a wonderful way to serve Christ. But by living, he would get to labor for Christ more on earth, producing more Christians. He doesn't know which is better, and so he seems to place it in God's hands. It's a wonderful example of St. Ignatius' third type of person.

We close today with this marvelous passage from St. Paul's Letter to the Philippians.

Closing Prayer

My eager expectation and hope is that I shall not be put to shame in any way, but that with all boldness, now as always, Christ will be magnified in my body, whether by life or by death.

For to me life is Christ, and death is gain. If I go on living in the flesh, that means fruitful labor for me. And I do not know which I shall choose. I am caught between the two. I long to depart this life and be with Christ, [for] that is far better. Yet that I remain [in] the flesh is more necessary for your benefit. (Philippians 1:20-24)

Amen.

Day 18

The Second Week

Bible Passage: Mark 4:35-41

Welcome to Day 18 of *Ascending with Ignatius*. Today we come to the very last day of the Second Week of the Spiritual Exercises. In the Third Week, which begins tomorrow, we will reflect on the very frightening images of Jesus going through his passion and death, so today we look at the question of fear. We look at fear especially as an obstacle to discipleship.

Let us begin our session with part of today's Scripture passage.

Opening Prayer

In the name of the Father and of the Son and of the Holy Spirit.

On that day, as evening drew on, [Jesus] said to them, "Let us cross to the other side." Leaving the crowd, they took him with them in the boat just as he was. And other boats were with him. A violent squall came up and waves were breaking over the boat, so that it was already filling up. Jesus was in the stern, asleep on a cushion. They woke him and said to him, "Teacher, do you not care that we are perishing?" He woke up, rebuked the wind, and said to the sea, "Quiet! Be still!" The wind ceased and there was great calm. Then he asked them, "Why are you terrified? Do you not yet have faith?" (Mark 4:35-40)

Amen.

Reflection

I find it humorous that the Gospel writer wants to tell us that Jesus is "asleep on a cushion" (Mark 4:38). This little detail seems to rub salt in the wounds of these frightened disciples who shake him and say, "Do you not care that we are perishing?" (4:38). Jesus is asleep on a cushion to emphasize that he completely trusts in the providence of God. After he brings calm to the storm, Jesus says to the disciples, "Why are you terrified? Do you not yet have faith?" (3:40). What this tells us is that the opposite of faith is not disbelief but, rather, fear.

Fear is the opposite of faith. When we are afraid, we are not trusting in the providence of God. We don't trust that

God will take good care of us, and so our problem is that we lack faith. Faith and fear go together, and fear is perhaps the greatest obstacle to discipleship. All we have to do is look at the Nativity stories and see what an incredibly large role fear plays as an obstacle to discipleship. Even Mary seems to be in danger of being afraid because the angel Gabriel has to tell her, "Do not be afraid" (Luke 1:30). Why is that? Perhaps Gabriel knows that the only thing that might keep Mary from saying yes is fear. Then, in Matthew's Gospel, Joseph is told in a dream, "Do not be afraid to take Mary your wife into your home" (1:20). And again, back in Luke's Gospel, when Zechariah is told that John the Baptist will be his son, the angel says to Zechariah, "Do not be afraid" (1:13). Finally, when the angels visit the shepherds to tell them about the baby Jesus, they begin their message with "Do not be afraid" (2:10). Do not be afraid; do not be afraid; do not be afraid! Again and again, the disciples are told not to be afraid.

Let's look now at the end of Mark's Gospel. Most scholars believe that Mark's Gospel originally ended with Mark 16:8. The women were told to go and tell Peter and the others that Jesus had risen, and the last line of the Gospel is: "They said nothing to anyone, for they were afraid" (Mark 16:8). Some scholars think that Mark's Gospel ended this way on purpose because Mark was trying to tell his audience that fear was the biggest obstacle to being a Christian. The belief is that Mark's audience was being harassed and persecuted by the government and that some of Mark's audience was giving up the faith out of fear. So perhaps Mark ended his gospel with this cliff-hanger—with no one saying anything about Jesus' resurrection because of fear.

Isn't it also true that fear is one of our greatest obstacles to discipleship today? Fear is what we need to ask the Lord to free us from. Years ago, I had to fly a lot for my job. Sometimes I would have this fear of flying, especially when taking off. I felt like it was a terrible idea to put hundreds of people in this metal can and rise 30,000 feet into the air. One day, when we were taking off, we had a lot of turbulence, and I was afraid. I was convinced that the whole thing is going to go crashing into the ground. I looked over at the flight attendant in the front of the plane, and she was just sitting in her seat flipping the pages of a magazine. When I saw that, I knew I had nothing to fear. From then on, anytime I was afraid on a flight, all I would do was look at the flight attendants to see how bored they were during the takeoff, and I knew everything was going to be okay.

A while after that incident with the flight attendant, I was praying about something in my ministry that was frightening me. I don't even remember what it was now, but I was asking the Lord to take this fear from me. And I saw in my prayerful imagination, Jesus with a magazine casually flipping the pages again and again, smiling. Jesus wasn't mocking me or making fun of me. He was teasing me. It was as though he were asleep on a cushion. He was trying to tell me that I had nothing to fear. He was trying to say, "Mark, why are you afraid? Where is your faith?" And so, today I challenge you to pray about the question of fear. How does fear play a role in your life as a disciple? Might it be true that fear is an obstacle in your own discipleship?

Let's close with the reading from the Gospel once again.

Closing Prayer

On that day, as evening drew on, [Jesus] said to them, "Let us cross to the other side." Leaving the crowd, they took him with them in the boat just as he was. And other boats were with him. A violent squall came up and waves were breaking over the boat, so that it was already filling up. Jesus was in the stern, asleep on a cushion. They woke him and said to him, "Teacher, do you not care that we are perishing?" He woke up, rebuked the wind, and said to the sea, "Quiet! Be still!" The wind ceased and there was great calm. Then he asked them, "Why are you terrified? Do you not yet have faith?" (Mark 4:35-40)

Amen.

Day 19

The Third Week

Bible Passage: Matthew 21:1-11

Welcome to Day 19 of *Ascending with Ignatius*. Congratulations! You've made it to the end of the Second Week of the Spiritual Exercises. Today we begin the Third Week. Before we do, let's summarize the whole movement of the Spiritual Exercises.

Before we began the four weeks of the Exercises, there was a preparatory week that we call the Principle and Foundation, where we explored the question of why we were created. What was God up to when he created us? What is God's original grand vision for creating humankind and everything that exists? We then began the First Week, which was a reflection on sin and mercy. The Second Week followed—a reflection on the life of Christ and discipleship. The Third Week is a reflection on Christ's passion and death. And in the Fourth

Week, we will reflect on the resurrection of Christ, the descent of the Holy Spirit, and the Ascension. In the Fourth Week, we will also reflect on moving forward into the rest of our lives, which we sometimes call the Fifth Week.

Today we begin our reflection on the solemn and somber story of Jesus' passion and death. You can think of this week as Holy Week, starting with Palm Sunday and ending with the burial of Christ. You might want to try to have a sort of a Holy Week in your own life this week—a week that is a bit quieter, where your spirit is a little more solemn and reflective. Today we begin with the story of Palm Sunday, when Jesus makes his entry into Jerusalem. Our Scripture passage is Matthew 21:1-11.

Opening Prayer

In the name of the Father and of the Son and of the Holy Spirit.

When they drew near Jerusalem and came to Bethphage on the Mount of Olives, Jesus sent two disciples, saying to them, "Go into the village opposite you, and immediately you will find an ass tethered, and a colt with her. Untie them and bring them here to me. . . .

The disciples went and did as Jesus had ordered them. They brought the ass and the colt and laid their cloaks over them, and he sat upon them. The very large crowd spread their cloaks on the road, while others cut branches from the trees and strewed them on the road. The crowds preceding him and those following kept crying out and saying:

"Hosanna to the Son of David;
blessed is he who comes in the name of the Lord;
hosanna in the highest."

And when he entered Jerusalem the whole city was shaken and asked, "Who is this?" And the crowds replied, "This is Jesus the prophet, from Nazareth in Galilee." (Matthew 21:1-2, 6-11)

Amen.

Reflection

Palm Sunday is a most ironic day. On the one hand, one could argue that Palm Sunday was one of Jesus' most victorious days. "The whole city was shaken," the Gospel tells us (Matthew 21:10). The entire city of Jerusalem was shaking with excitement. They greeted him as they would greet a king: spreading their cloaks, waving branches, shouting out, "Hosanna! Hosanna to the king!" What a wonderful day for Jesus! On the other hand, when we celebrate Palm Sunday in Mass, we always pray and reflect over the entire

Gospel story from this moment all the way through the death of Jesus. I'm always struck by the irony of this day. These crowds, shouting in exultation and adulation, will soon be shouting, "Crucify him! Crucify him! Crucify him!" It's an incredibly stark contrast as Jesus' great victory turns into terrible humiliation.

Years ago I gave a workshop—I don't even remember where—and it went really well. I remember being very excited about how well it went; everyone was enthusiastic and praised me with all kinds of compliments. I was feeling pretty good about myself and felt like I had a great victory. A bit proud of myself, I went and gave another workshop somewhere else about a week later. This time, it didn't go well. It wasn't a complete disaster—they didn't shout "Crucify him!" or anything—but they didn't really connect with me. And as good as I felt after that first event, I felt terrible after that second one. I felt humiliated and ashamed of myself. Afterwards, I was praying about those two moments, and I felt the Lord very gently saying to me, "Mark, why don't you not take too much credit for your victories and not take too much blame for your failures either? Just come to the end of your day and give me what you've got, and then go to bed."

It reminds me of a saying of Pope St. John XXIII. Before he went to sleep at night, he used to say, "Lord, it's your Church. I'm going to bed." What if you and I adopted that spirit? What if you and I, every day, didn't take too much credit for the victories and didn't take too much blame for the failures either and, instead, just did the best we could, gave it to God, and went to bed?

In today's Gospel, perhaps Jesus enjoys the day—the jubilant spirit of the people of Jerusalem—but he seems also to be a little above it. He seems not to take it in too deeply, not identifying himself with this victory. Perhaps he knows already what's to come. So as disciples of Christ, let us model ourselves after Jesus. Let us model ourselves after the way that he accepts the victories and the defeats with grace, turning it all over to God at the end of each day.

Let us close with the same Scripture passage.

Closing Prayer

When they drew near Jerusalem and came to Bethphage on the Mount of Olives, Jesus sent two disciples, saying to them, "Go into the village opposite you, and immediately you will find an ass tethered, and a colt with her. Untie them and bring them here to me. . . .

The disciples went and did as Jesus had ordered them. They brought the ass and the colt and laid their cloaks over them, and he sat upon them. The very large crowd spread their cloaks on the road, while others cut branches from the trees and strewed them on the road. The crowds preceding him and those following kept crying out and saying:

"Hosanna to the Son of David;

    blessed is he who comes in the name of the Lord;

hosanna in the highest."

And when he entered Jerusalem the whole city was shaken and asked, "Who is this?" And the crowds replied, "This is Jesus the prophet, from Nazareth in Galilee." (Matthew 21:1-2, 6-11)

Amen.

Day 20

The Third Week

Bible Passages: John 13:1-17; Matthew 26:26-30

Welcome to Day 20 of *Ascending with Ignatius*. We are in the middle of the Third Week of the Spiritual Exercises, where we take a sober look at the passion and death of Christ. Today I recommend we look at the washing of the feet and at the Eucharist. St. John's Gospel tells the story of the washing of the feet, and this seems to have happened at the very supper that came to be called the Eucharist. So I recommend we look at these stories together today. This involves reflecting on two Scripture passages: John 13:1-17 and Matthew 26:26-30.

Let us begin by reflecting on some excerpts from John's Gospel.

Opening Prayer

In the name of the Father and of the Son and of the Holy Spirit.

Jesus knew that his hour had come to pass from this world to the Father. He loved his own in the world and he loved them to the end. . . . He rose from supper and took off his outer garments. He took a towel and tied it around his waist. Then he poured water into a basin and began to wash the disciples' feet and dry them with the towel around his waist. . . .

So when he had washed their feet [and] put his garments back on and reclined at table again, he said to them, "Do you realize what I have done for you? You call me 'teacher' and 'master,' and rightly so, for indeed I am. If I, therefore, the master and teacher, have washed your feet, you ought to wash one another's feet. I have given you a model to follow, so that as I have done for you, you should also do." (John 13:1, 4-5, 12-15)

Amen.

Reflection

What would you do if you knew you had only twenty-four hours to live? Perhaps you would jump out of an airplane with a parachute or maybe you would go to the finest restaurant and order an extravagant meal or maybe you would do some grand gesture for your beloved.

What did Jesus choose to do with his last twenty-four hours? He was the divine Messiah, you know; he could have done some pretty incredible things with those last hours. But he chose the simplest gestures of all: he washed up his little ones, and he fed them a simple meal.

Surely Jesus was planting the seeds of our sacrament of the Eucharist in his words "This is my body" (Matthew 26:26) and through those gestures. Perhaps he was saying "This is my body" about these simple acts of love, these concrete gestures of service—washing up our little ones and feeding them a meal. "I'm in this," Jesus says. "My body is present in this." In doing these simple gestures, he consecrates them, making them sacred acts for the rest of us.

Pope Francis says that the coronavirus crisis has given us the opportunity to strip ourselves of the superfluous things of our lives and to cultivate the things that matter most.[7] We probably think of doing things like washing up our little kids and feeding them a meal as superfluous gestures, and yet Francis is correct. These are in fact the things that matter, and even if we don't have little ones who are our biological children, all of us are called to do what Jesus did. Whoever our little ones are—whoever the souls are that God has given us to care for in some tender way—you and I are called to metaphorically wash their feet and feed them.

It's very simple. Jesus is not asking an extraordinary thing here; he wants us to do the most basic acts of love. And in the final twenty-four hours before he died, he consecrated these acts. These simple gestures can be done any day of our life, whether we are stuck inside our house, whether we are happy or sad, whether we have a tremendous amount of resources or none at all. We can perform these simple gestures and, in the process, participate in the consecrated acts of Christ.

Let us close with another reading of today's Scripture passage.

Closing Prayer

Jesus knew that his hour had come to pass from this world to the Father. He loved his own in the world and he loved them to the end. . . . He rose from supper and took off his outer garments. He took a towel and tied it around his waist. Then he poured water into a basin and began to wash the disciples' feet and dry them with the towel around his waist. . . .

So when he had washed their feet [and] put his garments back on and reclined at table again, he said to them, "Do you realize what I have done for you? You call me 'teacher' and 'master,' and rightly so, for indeed I am. If I, therefore, the master and teacher, have washed your feet, you ought to wash one another's feet. I have given you a model to follow, so that as I have done for you, you should also do." (John 13:1, 4-5, 12-15)

Amen.

Day 21

The Third Week

Bible Passage: Matthew 27:15-50

Welcome to Day 21 of *Ascending with Ignatius*. We are in the middle of the Third Week of the Spiritual Exercises, where we pray over the passion and death of Christ. Today, we reflect on the very moment that Jesus dies and the hours leading up to it. Today I recommend you pray over Matthew 27:15-50.

Let us begin by prayerfully reading the passage.

Opening Prayer

In the name of the Father and of the Son and of the Holy Spirit.

Now on the occasion of the feast the governor was accustomed to release to the crowd one prisoner whom they wished. And at that time they had a notorious prisoner called [Jesus] Barabbas. So when they had assembled, Pilate said to them, "Which one do you want me to release to you, [Jesus] Barabbas, or Jesus called Messiah?" . . . They answered, "Barabbas!" Pilate said to them, "Then what shall I do with Jesus called Messiah?" They all said, "Let him be crucified!" But he said, "Why? What evil has he done?" They only shouted the louder, "Let him be crucified!". . . Then he released Barabbas to them, but after he had Jesus scourged, he handed him over to be crucified.

Then the soldiers of the governor took Jesus inside the praetorium and gathered the whole cohort around him. They stripped off his clothes and threw a scarlet military cloak about him. Weaving a crown out of thorns, they placed it on his head, and a reed in his right hand. And kneeling before him, they mocked him, saying, "Hail, King of the Jews!" They spat upon him and took the reed and kept striking him on the head. And when they had mocked him, they stripped him of the cloak, dressed him in his own clothes, and led him off to crucify him. . . .

After they had crucified him, they divided his garments by casting lots; then they sat down and kept watch over him there. And they placed over his head the written charge against him: This is Jesus, the King of the Jews. . . . Those passing by reviled him, shaking their heads and saying, "You who would destroy the temple and rebuild it in three days, save yourself, if you are the Son of God, [and] come down from the cross!" Likewise the chief priests with the scribes and elders mocked him and said, "He saved others; he cannot save himself. So he is the king of Israel! Let him come down from the cross now, and we will believe in him. He trusted in God; let him deliver him now if he wants him. For he said, 'I am the Son of God.'" The revolutionaries who were crucified with him also kept abusing him in the same way.

From noon onward, darkness came over the whole land until three in the afternoon. And about three o'clock Jesus cried out in a loud voice, "*Eli, Eli, lema sabachthani?*" which means, "My God, my God, why have you forsaken me?" . . . Jesus cried out again in a loud voice, and gave up his spirit. (Matthew 27:15-17, 21-23, 26-31, 35-37, 39-46, 50)

Amen.

Reflection

Today we pray over the very worst moments of Jesus' short life. These are most horrific events. But Jesus seems to have made his peace with these terrible experiences. He seems to have made his peace with his destiny long before this travesty. Back at the Transfiguration, he told Peter and the others that they would go to Jerusalem, where Jesus would be mocked, arrested, abused, beaten, and killed. He said it again and again, seeming to be making his peace with these things that were about to happen. Luke's Gospel says that

Jesus "set his face" towards Jerusalem (Luke 9:51, RSVCE). This phrase, found also in the suffering servant prophesies of Isaiah ("I have set my face like flint," Isaiah 50:7), signals a fierce and unwavering determination to accomplish his mission, despite being harshly treated.

Perhaps you and I, reflecting on these horrific days of when Jesus' worst fears came to light, could also make our own peace with the things that frighten us. Perhaps we can make our peace with the terrible futures that we sometimes have nightmares about.

Years ago, when I was a leader in an organization, I had to make a decision that was unpopular. One of the people who was affected by the decision turned against me and was sort of scheming behind my back. A friend of mine told me that this person was trying to look for ways to make me look bad. He was watching me to see if I would trip up somehow so he could use that against me. This had never happened to me before, and it was a terrible experience.

I went into my eight-day retreat that year with this frightening burden on my mind. Strangely enough, I began the retreat with a spirit of peace, and prayed over Psalm 23: "The LORD is my shepherd; / there is nothing I lack. / . . . to still waters he leads me. / . . . You set a table before me" (23:1, 2, 5). For a couple of days, I prayed over this one passage, and I imagined myself in a beautiful green pasture, with a little river running by. And Jesus was there, next to a picnic table, where he had set this wonderful spread before me. It was filled with Cajun delights like boudin, sauce piquant, and fricassee; and there were desserts like beignets and bread pudding. It was a marvelous meal! All of this made me smile and reflect on how much God has blessed me.

But as the days went on, my mind turned back to the man who was trying to undermine me. Reading Psalm 23 again, I noticed that it actually says, "You set a table before me / *in front of my enemies*" (23:5, emphasis mine). And so, when I went back to my picnic table the next day in prayer and partook of this wonderful spread, I noticed some bushes over by the river, and in the bushes were two eyes staring back at me. It was the man who was set against me. With a sinister look on his face, he was watching me, waiting to pounce. So this wonderful, pleasant, and peaceful scene turned frightening and foreboding. But suddenly grace came to my aid and I grabbed an extra plate and filled it with food. I walked over to the bush and handed the plate to the man. "Listen," I said, "you must be hungry with all of that stalking you're doing. I've got more food than I can possibly eat, so why don't you have some?" And I walked back to the table.

After another minute or two, I went back to the bushes and said, "You can get a better view by just sitting at the table with me. There's plenty of room and plenty of food. Why don't you come over and have a meal with me?"

Then the vision ended. I never got to see if the man would take me up on my offer to eat together. But inside myself I felt a great peace. I made peace with my frightening boogeyman in the bushes. I made peace with my nightmare.

Christ is calling each one of us to make peace with our nightmares; to make peace with suffering, with insults, with heartbreak, and even with death. Here in the Third Week, we pray about these sober and somber thoughts. We pray about suffering, death, and rejection. Let us look at Jesus and the way that he faced his own worst nightmares. And let us pray to Jesus that we too might make our peace. Pray that we may, if you will, offer a meal to our boogeyman—whether it's a person, an event, or whatever we are afraid might happen to us someday. Let us make peace with it. Let us set our face like flint towards our suffering, knowing that Christ has been there before us.

Let us close with our Scripture passage.

Closing Prayer

Now on the occasion of the feast the governor was accustomed to release to the crowd one prisoner whom they wished. And at that time they had a notorious prisoner called [Jesus] Barabbas. So when they had assembled, Pilate said to them, "Which one do you want me to release to you, [Jesus] Barabbas, or Jesus called Messiah?" . . . They answered, "Barabbas!" Pilate said to them, "Then what shall I do with Jesus called Messiah?" They all said, "Let him be crucified!" But he said, "Why? What evil has he done?" They only shouted the louder, "Let him be crucified!". . . Then he released Barabbas to them, but after he had Jesus scourged, he handed him over to be crucified.

Then the soldiers of the governor took Jesus inside the praetorium and gathered the whole cohort around him. They stripped off his clothes and threw a scarlet military cloak about him. Weaving a crown out of thorns, they placed it on his head, and a reed in his right hand. And kneeling before him, they mocked him, saying, "Hail, King of the Jews!" They spat upon him and took the reed and kept striking him on the head. And when they had mocked him, they stripped him of the cloak, dressed him in his own clothes, and led him off to crucify him. . . .

After they had crucified him, they divided his garments by casting lots; then they sat down and kept watch over him there. And they placed over his head the written charge against him: This is Jesus, the King of the Jews. . . . Those passing by reviled him, shaking their heads and saying, "You who would destroy the temple and rebuild it in three days, save yourself, if you are the Son of God, [and] come down from the cross!" Likewise the chief priests with the scribes and elders mocked him and said, "He saved others; he cannot save himself. So he is the king of Israel! Let him come down from the cross now, and we will believe in him. He trusted in God; let him deliver him now if he wants him. For he said, 'I am the Son of God.'" The revolutionaries who were crucified with him also kept abusing him in the same way.

From noon onward, darkness came over the whole land until three in the afternoon. And about three o'clock Jesus cried out in a loud voice, "*Eli, Eli, lema sabachthani?*" which means, "My God, my God, why have you forsaken me?" . . . Jesus cried out again in a loud voice, and gave up his spirit. (Matthew 27:15-17, 21-23, 26-31, 35-37, 39-46, 50)

Amen.

Day 22

The Third Week

Bible Passage: John 14:1-6

Welcome to Day 22 of *Ascending with Ignatius*. Today is the last day of the Third Week of the Spiritual Exercises. We have been reflecting on the passion and death of Christ. Today we reflect on Holy Saturday, when Jesus was in the tomb. It is a quiet day when we reflect on what it all was for. Why did Jesus come to live among us in the first place? Why did he choose to live, to suffer, and to die for us? What was his purpose? What was his vision?

Let us reflect today on John 14:1-6.

Opening Prayer

In the name of the Father and of the Son and of the Holy Spirit.

"Do not let your hearts be troubled. You have faith in God; have faith also in me. In my Father's house there are many dwelling places. If they were not, would I have told you that I am going to prepare a place for you? And if I go and prepare a place for you, I will come back again and take you to myself, so that where I am you also may be. Where [I] am going you know the way." Thomas said to him, "Master, we do not know where you are going; how can we know the way?" Jesus said to him, "I am the way and the truth and the life." (John 14:1-6)

Amen.

Reflection

Why did Jesus come? What was his purpose for living, suffering, and dying for us? For Ignatius, the purpose of the Third Week is to look upon Jesus and see all that he did for us out of love. So the obvious answer to the question of why Jesus came is that he loves us. But how does he love us through these particular events—his birth, life, suffering, and dying? In what way is this loving us?

I was a novice master for a while, in charge of young Jesuit seminarians. Part of this role was to send novices on short missions. These missions would last anywhere from a couple of weeks to several months, and some of them were a bit frightening and difficult. We would send them to poor countries and place them in precarious situations to see if they could indeed live this life of a Jesuit missionary.

One of my colleagues, another novice director, shared with me about a moment when his novices were nervous about their next assignment. He used this same passage from John 14 that we're reflecting on today. The novice master told the young Jesuits that Jesus' words—"I am going to prepare a place for you" (14:2)—are true every day of our lives. Jesus always goes before us and prepares a place for us, in every situation. You and I only dwell in the present, but Jesus dwells in the past, the present, and the future. And in the future, Jesus goes ahead of us at every stage of our lives. He prepares a place for us. Perhaps that's one way of looking at why Jesus came—to prepare a place for us in every aspect of our living, our suffering, and our dying.

When we reflect on the Incarnation, St. Ignatius says we are to imagine the Trinity looking down at the earth, seeing all the people. Some are living joyfully while others are miserable. The Holy Trinity says, "We must go to them." God seemed to want to participate in our lives. And the Holy Trinity, through Jesus, goes to each moment in the spectrum of life. Running the gamut of human experience, Jesus' own presence at each moment blesses and consecrates those moments for us. Jesus does this with every moment of life, but he especially does it now in the rejection, the mockery, the scorn, the suffering, and the death. Jesus wanted to be there first, to prepare a place for you and me. That is why he came. That is why he suffered and died. He was preparing a place for us in those hard moments of human existence.

It has been said that Jesus did not come to take away our suffering but to fill it with his presence. As you and I face our worst nightmares; as you and I face diminishment, heartbreak, and rejection; as we face suffering and finally death; we can remember that Jesus has gone ahead of us and prepared a place for us. And not just in heaven—yes, that too, which will be wonderful! But he has even prepared a place for us in these hard moments. We can have our peace with whatever comes to us, both in life and in death.

Let us close with our passage in prayer.

Closing Prayer

"Do not let your hearts be troubled. You have faith in God; have faith also in me. In my Father's house there are many dwelling places. If they were not, would I have told you that I am going to prepare a place for you? And if I go and prepare a place for you, I will come back again and take you to myself, so that where I am you also may be. Where [I] am going you know the way." Thomas said to him, "Master, we do not know where you are going; how can we know the way?" Jesus said to him, "I am the way and the truth and the life." (John 14:1-6)

Amen.

Day 23

The Fourth Week

Bible Passage: John 20:1-9

Welcome to Day 23 of *Ascending with Ignatius*, and congratulations! You've made it to the Fourth Week of the Spiritual Exercises.

Let's once again review the movements of the Spiritual Exercises of St. Ignatius before moving into the Fourth Week. First, we had a few days of preparation called the Principle and Foundation. In this period, we looked at our creation, seeing that God has created us in love. We reflected on God's ultimate vision for us and for all of creation. Then we moved into the First Week, where we explored our own sin and celebrated God's great mercy. Then we journeyed through the Second Week, looking at the life of Christ up to but not including his passion. In the Third Week, we looked at the passion and death of Christ, and now we arrive at the Fourth

Week. Here we look at the resurrection of Christ, his ascension into heaven, the descent of the Holy Spirit, and beyond. Jesuits sometimes refer to our life beyond the Spiritual Exercises as the Fifth Week.

Today's passage is John 20:1-9.

Opening Prayer

In the name of the Father and of the Son and of the Holy Spirit.

On the first day of the week, Mary of Magdala came to the tomb early in the morning, while it was still dark, and saw the stone removed from the tomb. So she ran and went to Simon Peter and to the other disciple whom Jesus loved, and told them, "They have taken the Lord from the tomb, and we don't know where they put him." So Peter and the other disciple went out and came to the tomb. . . . When Simon Peter arrived . . . , he went into the tomb and saw the burial cloths there, and the cloth that had covered his head, not with the burial cloths but rolled up in a separate place. Then the other disciple also went in, . . . and he saw and believed. For they did not yet understand the scripture that he had to rise from the dead. (John 20:1-3, 6-9)

Amen.

Reflection

Note how the resurrection begins in a low-key way. Jesus does not burst onto the scene and say, "Tada!" when he rises from the dead. Instead, we have a quiet, sort of incremental revelation of the resurrected Jesus. In fact, we don't see the resurrected Jesus at all in the first scenes of the resurrection. In all four Gospels, the stories of the resurrection begin not with the resurrected Jesus but with the empty tomb. This is important because it gives us a message about our own experiences of resurrection.

When we go through some experience of loss—when we are down, we fail, we lose a loved one, or some other terrible thing happens to us—Jesus wants to bring resurrection into our lives. Perhaps, though, it won't begin with a burst onto the scene but, rather, with simply an incremental step—an empty tomb. In other words, the experience of the resurrection for you and me might begin not so much with resurrection but with a lack of death—the fact that we are still alive, that we still wake up in the morning. This is how we begin our Fourth Week, in this low-key way. Before we look at the resurrected Jesus, we look simply at an empty tomb.

John's Gospel is very carefully written. Every word is important, and every detail symbolic, trying to tell us something. In today's passage, John says that they went to the tomb "while it was still dark" (20:1). For John, darkness is always a symbol that we do not see and believe quite yet.

It indicates a lack of enlightenment, a lack of knowledge. When they find the empty tomb, for example, the women run to Peter and say, "They have taken the Lord . . . , and we *don't know* where they put him" (John 20:2, emphasis mine). They don't know; they don't understand. Even at the end of the story, when Peter and the other disciple find the empty tomb, it doesn't say that they received a complete revelation. Rather, they saw and believed even though "they did not yet understand" (20:9).

Perhaps John is trying to tell us about this incremental revelation of the resurrected Jesus. When we experience a loss or death, whether it's the literal death of our loved one or some other kind of loss, the beginnings of a resurrection might be a type of "empty tomb"—some small, indirect symbol of hope.

When I was in Israel, I discovered that the Church of the Holy Sepulchre, which is the church where the empty tomb of Jesus sits, is one of the most sacred places in Israel and in the entire Christian Church. It's one of the most sacred places in the world. I had the great privilege of spending an entire night in vigil at the empty tomb. At one moment, I got a marvelous revelation when I realized that this holy site is different from any other holy site in the world because it is revered, not for what is there, but for what is not there. There is a tomb, but there is no dead body. We Christians, even today, do not have a resurrected body to show the world when we tell the story of our faith. But we do have our little empty tombs, our little places where death should be but is not; signs—even if only flickers—of hope.

When I was a novice director, I saw that one of the novices was struggling, though he still had hope within him. I asked him, "Do you sense that the Lord seems far away from you?" He said, "Well, the Lord is not near, but he's not far either." That's precisely where our flickers of hope are often found. We don't have a sense of Jesus being near, but we know that he's not far either. This is an important message in times of crisis. We may feel as though the Lord is not near; he is in fact near, but we often don't feel his nearness during the dark and difficult days. But we also know that he's not far either.

St. Peter tells us to "always be ready to give an explanation to anyone who asks you for a reason for your hope" (1 Peter 3:15). We should always be ready to explain the hope that is within us. It's these little flickers of hope that are important. It's wonderful when we feel euphoric joy and immense consolation, and these moments are powerful revelations of the resurrected Jesus in our lives. But at other times, resurrection begins in a slow, quiet, and incremental way. There's just a flicker of hope, not a raging fire. The Lord is asking us to be ready to give an explanation to the world for our Christian hope—even if, at the moment, it is just a flicker of light or an empty tomb.

We close by once again reflecting on our passage.

Closing Prayer

On the first day of the week, Mary of Magdala came to the tomb early in the morning, while it was still dark, and saw the stone removed from the tomb. So she ran and went to Simon Peter and to the other disciple whom Jesus loved, and told them, "They have taken the Lord from the tomb, and we don't know where they put him." So Peter and the other disciple went out and came to the tomb. . . . When Simon Peter arrived . . . , he went into the tomb and saw the burial cloths there, and the cloth that had covered his head, not with the burial cloths but rolled up in a separate place. Then the other disciple also went in, . . . and he saw and believed. For they did not yet understand the scripture that he had to rise from the dead. (John 20:1-3, 6-9)

Amen.

Day 24

The Fourth Week

Bible Passages: John 20:11-18; John 20:24-29

Welcome to Day 24 of our thirty-day retreat. We are in the early days of the Fourth Week of the Spiritual Exercises, where we joyfully reflect on the resurrection of Jesus Christ.

Today I recommend that you reflect on two Scripture passages, both from the twentieth chapter of John's Gospel: the story of Mary of Magdala in verses 11-18 and the story of Thomas in verses 24-29. We will use the second passage, the wonderful story of Jesus inviting Thomas to touch his wounds, for our opening prayer.

Opening Prayer

In the name of the Father and of the Son and of the Holy Spirit.

Thomas, called Didymus, one of the Twelve, was not with them when Jesus came. So the other disciples said to him, "We have seen the Lord." But he said to them, "Unless I see the mark of the nails in his hands and put my finger into the nailmarks and put my hand into his side, I will not believe." Now a week later his disciples were again inside and Thomas was with them. Jesus came, although the doors were locked, and stood in their midst and said, "Peace be with you." Then he said to Thomas, "Put your finger here and see my hands, and bring your hand and put it into my side, and do not be unbelieving, but believe." Thomas answered and said to him, "My Lord and my God!" (John 20:24-28)

Amen.

Reflection

St. Ignatius, in the Fourth Week of the Spiritual Exercises, has a unique way of inviting us to think about Jesus. He says in the Fourth Week, "Consider the office of consoler that Christ our Lord exercises, and compare it with the way in which friends are wont to console each other."[8] This is the lens through which St. Ignatius would like you to read all of these wonderful resurrection stories. Jesus comes as a consoler.

In the Gospel stories before the resurrection, Jesus is most often found speaking to groups, to crowds, or to the disciples gathered together. He of course speaks with people individually as well, but in the resurrection stories, he seems more than ever to go to each individual. Jesus consoles each one of his friends in the particular way that helps them. This is what good friends do.

Look at the stark contrast between how Jesus consoled Thomas and Mary of Magdala. To Thomas, Jesus says, in effect, "Come and touch me; touch my wounds." He's encouraging Thomas to come close and touch him physically. But he says to Mary Magdalene just before that, "Stop holding on to me" (John 20:17). Wait a minute. Why does he give two opposite instructions? Why does he ask his two friends to do the completely opposite thing? It's because Jesus knows what each of them needs. He knows that, in order to be consoled, Mary actually needs to stop clinging, to let go. Thomas needs to come close and perhaps touch him in his wounds.

We see a third type of response with the Emmaus disciples in Luke 24. Joining them in their walk from Jerusalem to Emmaus, Jesus explains the Scriptures to these disheartened believers. He shows them the theological underpinnings of his resurrection, which he doesn't do with anyone else. Perhaps they were deep thinkers who needed this particular consolation of biblical theology. They needed an explanation. I like to think of these two Emmaus Road disciples as bookish Jesuits!

St. Peter, on the other hand, is a man of action. He doesn't need the theological explanation. What he needs is an abundant catch of fish to console him because he knows that Jesus is present when there is abundance.

Jesus seems to go to each individual and to care for their particular needs. In the Society of Jesus (the Jesuits), we call this concept *cura personalis*. It's a Latin phrase for personal care, meaning that we try to understand and console people as friends console one another—tending to their particular wants and needs.

Jesus seems to live out this *cura personalis*, but take note of one thing: Jesus doesn't always give us what we want, but he always gives us what we need. That's true for our friends as well, right? Sometimes we ask of our friends something that we want but that isn't necessarily good for us. A true friend might say, "No, I'm going to give you what you need instead." Peter, for example, wants to go back to his profession of fishing, but Jesus steers him away from that and back to being a shepherd for the church. "It's not fish, Peter; it's sheep I want you going after."

The Emmaus disciples are heading out of town, but Jesus turns them around, sending them back to Jerusalem. Mary Magdalene wants to cling when Jesus knows she needs to let go. We don't even know if Thomas really needed to touch Jesus' wounds; the story ends before he actually touches him. Perhaps Thomas just needed Jesus to make the offer, and that was enough for him. We all sometimes express our desires to Christ, as well we should. But we should also know that Christ will give us what we need, not what we want.

Thomas gets a bad rap for demanding from Jesus to touch his wounds, but he shouldn't. St. Ignatius says that all of us should begin our prayer asking for particular graces. I think Ignatius would have liked Thomas because he had the boldness to ask Jesus for the things that he needed. Ignatius would want us to do the same.

Perhaps in this resurrection period of our retreat, you can ponder the question: What do I need in order to see and believe?

- Do I need to cling tighter to Jesus, like Thomas?

- Or, like Mary, do I need to let go of my old notions of Jesus and learn something new?

- Do I need some sort of sign of abundance in my life, like Peter's catch of fish?

- Do I need some theological understanding, like the Emmaus disciples?

What do you need? What do you personally need in order to experience the risen Christ?

In this Fourth Week of the Exercises, go to Jesus, and tell him what you think you need. Tell him what it is that you desire. But be open to Jesus doing what you really need instead of what you might think you need. Tell him what you need; then stay open to however he chooses to come to you.

Let us close by reading our Scripture passage once again.

Closing Prayer

Thomas, called Didymus, one of the Twelve, was not with them when Jesus came. So the other disciples said to him, "We have seen the Lord." But he said to them, "Unless I see the mark of the nails in his hands and put my finger into the nailmarks and put my hand into his side, I will not believe." Now a week later his disciples were again inside and Thomas was with them. Jesus came, although the doors were locked, and stood in their midst and said, "Peace be with you." Then he said to Thomas, "Put your finger here and see my hands, and bring your hand and put it into my side, and do not be unbelieving, but believe." Thomas answered and said to him, "My Lord and my God!" (John 20:24-28)

Amen.

Day 25

The Fourth Week

Bible Passages: Luke 24:13-35; Acts 8:26-40

Welcome to Day 25 of *Ascending with Ignatius*. We are in the Fourth Week of the Spiritual Exercises, where we joyfully reflect on the stories of the resurrected Jesus. Today we will reflect on two passages. One of them is what you might expect, and the other is perhaps a bit of a surprise. Luke 24:13-35 is the wonderful story of the disciples encountering Jesus on the road to Emmaus, and Acts of the Apostles 8:26-40 is the story of Philip after the Ascension, encountering an Ethiopian eunuch on a road. The eunuch encounters the risen Lord through the testimony of Philip and through Baptism.

We begin with the road to Emmaus.

Opening Prayer

In the name of the Father and of the Son and of the Holy Spirit.

Now that very day two of them were going to a village seven miles from Jerusalem called Emmaus, and they were conversing about all the things that had occurred. And it happened that while they were conversing and debating, Jesus himself drew near and walked with them, but their eyes were prevented from recognizing him. He asked them, "What are you discussing as you walk along?" They stopped, looking downcast. One of them, named Cleopas, said to him in reply, "Are you the only visitor to Jerusalem who does not know of the things that have taken place there in these days?" And he replied to them, "What sort of things?" They said to him, "The things that happened to Jesus the Nazarene, who was a prophet mighty in deed and word before God and all the people, how our chief priests and rulers both handed him over to a sentence of death and crucified him. But we were hoping that he would be the one to redeem Israel; and besides all this, it is now the third day since this took place. Some women from our group, however, have astounded us: they were at the tomb early in the morning and did not find his body; they came back and reported that they had indeed seen a vision of angels who announced that he was alive. Then some of those with us went to the tomb and found things just as the women had described, but him they did not see." And he said to them, "Oh, how foolish you are! How slow of heart to believe all that the prophets spoke! Was it not necessary that the Messiah should suffer these things and enter into his glory?" Then beginning with Moses and all the prophets, he interpreted to them what referred to him in all the scriptures. As they approached the village to which they were going, he gave the impression that he was going on farther. But they urged him, "Stay with us, for it is nearly evening and the day is almost over." So he went in to stay with them. And it happened that, while he was with them at table, he took bread, said the blessing, broke it, and gave it to them. With that their eyes were opened and they recognized him, but he vanished from their sight. Then they said to each other, "Were not our hearts burning [within us] while he spoke to us on the way and opened the scriptures to us?" So they set out at once and returned to Jerusalem where they found gathered together the eleven and those with them who were saying, "The Lord has truly been raised and has appeared to Simon!" Then the two recounted what had taken place on the way and how he was made known to them in the breaking of the bread. (Luke 24:13-35)

Amen.

Reflection

Today I would like you to reflect on the spiritual phenomenon that is symbolized in this story of the road to Emmaus. Oftentimes we encounter the Lord not where we might think he should be but, instead, in between things, on the way from one thing to another. Jerusalem was the holy place, the center of all the religious activity. But after the tragic end to Jesus' life in Jerusalem, these two disciples leave the holy city and travel back to Emmaus. And on that road, going away from where Jesus is supposed to be, they encounter him. We see this same phenomenon in the story from Acts, when Philip encounters the eunuch. The eunuch encounters the risen Lord on the road, on the way, in between things. And even the women of the tomb in Matthew's Gospel are coming back from the tomb, traveling towards the Upper Room when they meet Jesus on the road.

Perhaps the Gospel writers are trying to tell us that we too will often encounter the risen Lord, not where we think we might find him, but on the road and in between things. Perhaps it's in the transition from one phase of life to another, or perhaps it's not at some big moments that we think are the most important of our lives but in the ordinary moments in between.

In the resurrection stories, Jesus not only tends to appear in these in-between places, but he often has an ordinary appearance. They think he's the gardener at one time. Another time, he seems to be just another guy on the street or at the beach. Jesus is trying to tell you and me to look for him not only in the sacred places that look like they're holy, but in the ordinary moments and people of our day as well.

When I was a novice director, I would guide the new Jesuits on their thirty-day silent retreats. I would tell them not only to look for Jesus in those precise moments of prayer, but not to be surprised if they have the most important encounters in between those prayer times. When they would come to see me every day and talk about their retreat, they would surely tell me about their wonderful moments in prayer.

But every now and then, when I asked the question "What was the most important moment of your day?" they would talk about the in-between moments. It could be on the way to the dining room or perhaps while brushing their teeth, in the shower, or exercising on a bicycle. It was in these most ordinary moments of the day that they encountered the Lord.

I invite you to reflect on this phenomenon in your own life. Do you ever expect to find Jesus in some particular place but find him on the road instead? Are you ever like the Emmaus disciples, expecting to find Jesus in Jerusalem but then giving up hope there, only to find him outside of Jerusalem after all? Sometimes Jesus dwells where we least expect to find him. Sometimes he wears the face of a gardener—someone we weren't thinking of as Christ. How has the resurrected Lord surprised you with an appearance "on the road" and "in between"?

Let us close by returning to our passage.

Closing Prayer

Now that very day two of them were going to a village seven miles from Jerusalem called Emmaus, and they were conversing about all the things that had occurred. And it happened that while they were conversing and debating, Jesus himself drew near and walked with them, but their eyes were prevented from recognizing him. He asked them, "What are you discussing as you walk along?" They stopped, looking downcast. One of them, named Cleopas, said to him in reply, "Are you the only visitor to Jerusalem who does not know of the things that have taken place there in these days?" And he replied to them, "What sort of things?" They said to him, "The things that happened to Jesus the Nazarene, who was a prophet mighty in deed and word before God and all the people, how our chief priests and rulers both handed him over to a sentence of death and crucified him. But we were hoping that he would be the one to redeem Israel; and besides all this, it is now the third day since this took place. Some women from our group, however, have astounded us: they were at the tomb early in the morning and did not find his body; they came back and reported that they had indeed seen a vision of angels who announced that he was alive. Then some of those with us went to the tomb and found things just as the women had described, but him they did not see." And he said to them, "Oh, how foolish you are! How slow of heart to believe all that the prophets spoke! Was it not necessary that the Messiah should suffer these things and enter into his glory?" Then beginning with Moses and all the prophets, he interpreted to them what referred to him in all the scriptures. As they approached the village to which they were going, he gave the impression that he was going on farther. But they urged him, "Stay with us, for it is nearly evening and the day is almost over." So he went in to stay with them. And it happened that, while he was with them at table, he took bread, said the blessing, broke it, and gave it to them. With that their eyes were opened and they recognized him, but he vanished from their sight. Then they said to each other, "Were not our hearts burning [within us] while he spoke to us on the way and opened the scriptures to us?" So they set out at once and returned to Jerusalem where they found gathered together the eleven and those with them who were saying, "The Lord has truly been raised and has appeared to Simon!" Then the two recounted what had taken place on the way and how he was made known to them in the breaking of the bread. (Luke 24:13-35)

Amen.

Day 26

The Fourth Week

Bible Passage: John 14:6-9

Welcome to Day 26 of *Ascending with Ignatius*. We are in the midst of the Fourth Week where we joyfully reflect on the resurrection of Christ. Today I have an unusual passage for you to reflect on: John 14:6-9. John 14 is part of what is called the "farewell discourses" of Jesus. They are the last things that Jesus said just before he was arrested in the Garden of Olives. The reason I invite you to reflect on this in the context of the resurrection is because many scholars believe that some or maybe all of these farewell discourses were actually preached after the resurrection. They claim that these are in fact resurrection discourses. If you read chapters 14 through 17 of John's Gospel, you'll see that they fit just as well in the resurrection context as they do before Jesus' death. It's interesting and enlightening to read them in both contexts.

First, read them as though Jesus were saying these words before his death, and then read them again as though Jesus were talking after his resurrection.

Let's begin with just a small portion of these farewell discourses.

Opening Prayer

In the name of the Father and of the Son and of the Holy Spirit.

Jesus said to [Thomas], . . . "If you know me, then you will also know my Father. From now on you do know him and have seen him." Philip said to him, "Master, show us the Father, and that will be enough for us." Jesus said to him, "Have I been with you for so long a time and you still do not know me, Philip? Whoever has seen me has seen the Father." (John 14:6, 7-9)

Amen.

Reflection

In today's passage, Philip asks Jesus to show us the Father. That request actually originates from the Old Testament when Moses asked God to reveal himself. Moses yearned to see God's face, as did Phillip, and as do you and I.

But when Moses made that request, he got a very different answer from God than Jesus gave. When Moses asked, "Please let me see your glory!" (Exodus 33:18), God replied, "You cannot see my face, for no one can see me and live" (33:20). This yearning in Moses, in Philip, and in you and me, comes from the yearning to return to Eden—to that wonderful place where we walked with the Father in the breezy times of the day. Moses is told that we cannot see the face of the Father. Why? Because we were expelled from the Garden of Eden. But Jesus answers in a different way: "Whoever has seen me has seen the Father" (John 14:9). In essence he says, "I am the face of the Father. You know the face of the Father because you know my face." What Jesus is saying is that through his life, death, and resurrection, we return to Eden—the place we've always longed for. It's our true home, where we know the face of the Father. Recall the original vision of God that we saw in the early days of the retreat— the Principle and Foundation. We see it again now. Jesus is saying that we now return to Eden, seeing again the face of the Father through the face of Christ.

When Moses asked God to tell him his name, God in effect told him, "You cannot know my name." He answers with "I am who I am" (Exodus 3:14)—Yahweh. Scripture scholars say this is a sort of a non-answer. We were not allowed to know the name of God because of our expulsion from Eden. But now, we know God's name through Jesus Christ. The name of God is the name of Jesus. In Jesus Christ, we know God's face and we know God's name. We return to Eden, walking with God again in the breezy parts of the day. This is the joy of Easter. This is the gift that God the Trinity has given us through the life, death, and resurrection of Jesus. Let us celebrate that today. Let us celebrate what Jesus's resurrection means—that we return to Eden and we can once again walk with God the Father as our close friend and companion.

Let us close once again with our Scripture passage.

Closing Prayer

Jesus said to [Thomas], . . . "If you know me, then you will also know my Father. From now on you do know him and have seen him." Philip said to him, "Master, show us the Father, and that will be enough for us." Jesus said to him, "Have I been with you for so long a time and you still do not know me, Philip? Whoever has seen me has seen the Father." (John 14:6, 7-9)

Amen.

Day 27

The Fourth Week

Bible Passage: John 21:1-14

Welcome to Day 27 of *Ascending with Ignatius*. We are in the Fourth Week of the Spiritual Exercises, reflecting on the beautiful passages of the resurrection. A couple of days ago, we discovered that we sometimes find the resurrected Jesus on the road and in the in-between moments of life. Today I suggest that we find the resurrected Lord in the midst of community. We find him in the bond between the people that God has given us to be with us in our lives. Our reflection today is from John 21:1-14.

Opening Prayer

In the name of the Father and of the Son and of the Holy Spirit.

After these things Jesus showed himself again to the disciples by the Sea of Tiberias; and he showed himself in this way. Gathered there together were Simon Peter, Thomas called the Twin, Nathanael of Cana in Galilee, the sons of Zebedee, and two others of his disciples. Simon Peter said to them, "I am going fishing." They said to him, "We will go with you." They went out and got into the boat, but that night they caught nothing.

Just after daybreak, Jesus stood on the beach; but the disciples did not know that it was Jesus. Jesus said to them, "Children, you have no fish, have you?" They answered him, "No." He said to them, "Cast the net to the right side of the boat, and you will find some." So they cast it, and now they were not able to haul it in because there were so many fish. That disciple whom Jesus loved said to Peter, "It is the Lord!" When Simon Peter heard that it was the Lord, he put on some clothes, for he was naked, and jumped into the sea. (John 21:1-7, NRSVCE)

Amen.

Reflection

Where do we find the resurrected Lord? In community. That's where Jesus wants to be found. What do I mean by community? Community is the people that God has called a person to be with. For the first disciples, community meant the whole group of Jesus' apostles and disciples. For me, my primary community is my Jesuit community. For most of us, community is the biological family that we live with, as well as the neighbors we live near, the church we go to, our workplace, and all the groups of people that God wants us to be with. That's where we will find Christ. And when we exit the community, we exit the presence of the resurrected Lord.

Let me show you how this is displayed in three of the resurrection stories.

First, we have the Emmaus story, which we saw two days ago. Discouraged by the events surrounding the crucifixion, the Emmaus disciples want to leave the community in Jerusalem. They lose hope and exit the community, setting out for Emmaus. Jesus comes up beside them, and their encounter with the resurrected Lord leads them back to their community in Jerusalem. We also see that they find the resurrected Lord "in the breaking of the bread" (Luke 24:35). This phrase would have had a special meaning for the Israelite people. One might say, "Joseph and I break bread together," meaning that the two of them are friends. So to say that Jesus was made known to them "in the breaking of the bread" means that they encounter Jesus in the gift of friendship, of community. In fact, the term *companion* comes from the Latin words for "with bread" (*cum* + *panis*—and in Spanish, *con pan*). So we find that these two disciples discovered the resurrected Lord in companionship.

The story of Thomas, which we saw on Day 24, also shows the resurrected Lord revealed in community, though it's easy to miss this subtle point. Just before the account of Thomas and the resurrected Jesus, it reads,

> On the evening of that first day of the week, when the doors were locked, where the disciples were, for fear of the Jews, Jesus came and stood in their midst and said to them, "Peace be with you." When he had said this, he showed them his hands and his side. The disciples rejoiced when they saw the Lord. [Jesus] said to them again, "Peace be with you. As the Father has sent me, so I send you." And when he had said this, he breathed on them and said to them, "Receive the holy Spirit."
>
> Thomas, called Didymus, one of the Twelve, was not with them when Jesus came. So the other disciples said to him, "We have seen the Lord." But he said to them, "Unless I see the mark of the nails in his hands and put my finger into the nailmarks and put my hand into his side, I will not believe." (John 20:19-22, 24-25)

Thomas "was not with them" (John 20:24). Remember that in John's Gospel, the details of the story often convey a symbolic message. It's not simply that Thomas went out to get some groceries. Thomas is a symbol of the Christian who has exited the community. Thomas exited the community; therefore, Thomas did not encounter the risen Lord. And look at all he missed! He missed the encounter with the risen Lord; he missed a double dose of peace, as twice Jesus said, "Peace be with you" (20:19, 21). Thomas also missed Jesus' commissioning: "As the Father has sent me, so I send you" (20:21). Outside of the companions he was called to be with, Thomas no longer has an identity, a mission in life. Is he still a disciple since he doesn't have a mission? That question is in play. Finally, it says that Jesus breathed on them and said, "Receive the holy Spirit" (20:22). So Thomas does not yet have the Holy Spirit.

Simply because Thomas had exited the community, he missed an encounter with the risen Lord that bestowed peace, a mission, and the Holy Spirit. It must have been a terrible week for him as all of the disciples were rejoicing over this life-changing encounter.

"Now a week later," the story continues, "his disciples were again inside and Thomas was with them" (John 20:26). I'll bet he was! I'll bet Thomas never left that room; he probably didn't go to the bathroom for a whole week because he wanted to be with the disciples so much! He got the lesson: if I exit the community, I leave the resurrected Lord. And when Jesus appears again, he invites Thomas to touch his wounds. The message here is as clear for us as it was for Thomas: if you exit community, you remove yourself from receiving the Holy Spirit and the gift of the resurrected Lord.

Let's look at one more resurrection story—today's passage telling of Peter's great catch. The story begins with Simon Peter saying, "I'm going fishing" (John 21:3, NRSVCE), and the others say, "We're going with you." What is happening here? Fishing is Peter's old life. It's what he did before Jesus, before the apostles, before this new community that he's been called to. His saying "I'm going fishing" is an exiting of the community, like Thomas and like the Emmaus disciples. But the disciples won't let him go off on his own. *Oh no, you're not leaving us; we're going with you.* They get in the boat with Peter, but they catch nothing that night, because they're not where they're supposed to be. Peter is trying to return to his old life, and it's not working out. Then Jesus, whom they don't recognize, standing on the shore, says, "Cast the net over the right side" (John 21:6). They have an abundant catch, and "the disciple whom Jesus loved," presumably John, said to Peter, "It is the Lord" (21:7). Upon hearing this, Peter put some clothes on and jumped into the sea.

Ponder for a moment: what if Peter had gone fishing alone? Peter did not recognize Jesus until John pointed him out. John seems to have a greater gift of discernment; he was able to discern the presence of Jesus. If Peter had exited the community as he wished, going out by himself, he may not have recognized the Lord.

But if Peter needed John, John also needed Peter. After hearing that it was the Lord, Peter jumped into the sea. John recognized the Lord, but he didn't jump in. Why not? Maybe John was blessed with the gift of discernment, but not as much with the gift of courage. This courage, strength, and bold-ness were Peter's gifts. Without Peter's courage, perhaps the others would have fled in fear, thinking Jesus was some sort of a ghost. My point is this: in order to encounter the risen Lord in this story, Peter needed John to discern the presence of Jesus, and John needed Peter to jump into the sea boldly and lead them back to the shore where Jesus was. The message is clear: it takes the entire community to recognize and approach the risen Lord.

We must not exit the community as Thomas and the Emmaus disciples did and as Peter tried to do. Instead, we must stay with community. Like the disciples, we must say, "We are going with you. We're not leaving you. We all need to stay together."

At the end of this story, it says that when they counted all the fish, there were 153 in number. Once again, no detail of John's Gospel is inconsequential—153 was the number of fish in the zodiac according to the Israelites. In other words, the Israelites thought that there were exactly 153 species of fish in the world. So to say that 153 fish were caught by this net, which was not torn, is to say that all of the world—every species, every creature—was scooped up. The community of Jesus is for everything and everyone.

Let us reflect on our own experience of encountering Christ in community, and how every time we exit community, when Christ has called us to be in community, we lose the risen Lord in the process.

We close by praying over our passage one more time.

Closing Prayer

After these things Jesus showed himself again to the disciples by the Sea of Tiberias; and he showed himself in this way. Gathered there together were Simon Peter, Thomas called the Twin, Nathanael of Cana in Galilee, the sons of Zebedee, and two others of his disciples. Simon Peter said to them, "I am going fishing." They said to him, "We will go with you." They went out and got into the boat, but that night they caught nothing.

Just after daybreak, Jesus stood on the beach; but the disciples did not know that it was Jesus. Jesus said to them, "Children, you have no fish, have you?" They answered him, "No." He said to them, "Cast the net to the right side of the boat, and you will find some." So they cast it, and now they were not able to haul it in because there were so many fish. That disciple whom Jesus loved said to Peter, "It is the Lord!" When Simon Peter heard that it was the Lord, he put on some clothes, for he was naked, and jumped into the sea. (John 21:1-7, NRSVCE)

Amen.

Day 28

The Fourth Week

Bible Passage: John 21:15-23

Welcome to Day 28. We're nearing the end of the retreat and celebrating the latter days of the Fourth Week as we relish the stories of the resurrection. Today I invite you to pray over the beautiful Gospel story of the conversation between Peter and Jesus on the beach, from John 21:15-23. As you do so, I encourage you to pray over the theme of mission. Just as we put on a dual lens during the Second Week when we prayed over the life of Christ along with the theme of discipleship, I encourage us to put on another dual lens today. As you pray over the resurrection of Jesus, pray also over the idea of mission: What is your mission, based on your experience of the risen Christ?

We'll begin by reading most of this passage as our opening prayer.

Opening Prayer

In the name of the Father and of the Son and of the Holy Spirit.

When they had finished breakfast, Jesus said to Simon Peter, "Simon, son of John, do you love me more than these?" He said to him, "Yes, Lord, you know that I love you." He said to him, "Feed my lambs." He then said to him a second time, "Simon, son of John, do you love me?" He said to him, "Yes, Lord, you know that I love you." He said to him, "Tend my sheep." He said to him the third time, "Simon, son of John, do you love me?" Peter was distressed that he had said to him a third time, "Do you love me?" and he said to him, "Lord, you know everything; you know that I love you." [Jesus] said to him, "Feed my sheep. Amen, amen, I say to you, when you were younger, you used to dress yourself and go where you wanted; but when you grow old, you will stretch out your hands, and someone else will dress you and lead you where you do not want to go." He said this signifying by what kind of death he would glorify God. And when he had said this, he said to him, "Follow me."

Peter turned and saw the disciple following whom Jesus loved, the one who had also reclined upon his chest during the supper. . . . When Peter saw him, he said to Jesus, "Lord, what about him?" Jesus said to him, "What if I want him to

remain until I come? What concern is it of yours? You follow me." (John 21:15-20, 21-22)

Amen.

Reflection

This beautiful scene is often referred to as Peter's first confession. Peter had to be absolved of his sin, not so much
for Jesus' sake, but for Peter to receive the recovery that he
needed in order to become the disciple Jesus was calling him
to be. In addition to this theme of healing, I also invite you
to notice how Jesus tells Peter to go. "Simon, son of John,
do you love me? . . . Feed my lambs. . . . Do you love me?
. . . Feed my sheep" (John 21:15, 17). There's an urgency
here; it's as if, grammatically, Jesus doesn't want these two
phrases to be outside of one sentence. They go together. "If
you love me, then you must feed my sheep." These things
cannot be separated.

Jesus is trying to point out this connection to Peter, even as
he's healing Peter of the wounds brought about by his terrible misstep of denying Christ. Yes, he's healing Peter because
he loves Peter; Jesus came to forgive our sins. But he's also
sending Peter into mission. He wants Peter to be a strong
disciple—an ambassador of the risen Lord. And Jesus knows
that this won't happen until Peter's soul is clean, until he's
healed so that he can move forward. A wounded warrior is
not going to be very effective. A runner with a rock in his

shoe is not going to run very far or very fast. So Jesus sets out to remove the rock from Peter's shoe so that he can run. In doing this, Jesus is saying that these two things—discipleship and mission—are inseparable. "Do you love me? Then go feed my sheep." You cannot do one without the other.

What about you and me? We do in fact have an exclusive relationship with Jesus, but only to an extent. If we really do love Jesus, our relationship with him is going to burst forth into ministry. Loving Jesus quite simply leads us to bring others to the resurrected Lord. It's the inevitable result of having an intimate relationship with Jesus. It's also what the Trinity did. Recall our reflection on the Trinity looking down at the earth and saying, "We must go to them." There's an urgency here, a demand that love makes: we must go to them in love. That same demand, which love makes even on the Trinity, is found here in Jesus' words to Peter. "Do you love me, Peter? Then go feed my sheep." It's the demand of love.

Jesus goes on to tell Peter, "When you were younger, you used to dress yourself and go where you wanted; but when you grow old, you will stretch out your hands, and someone else will dress you and lead you where you do not want to go" (John 21:18). Of course, John's Gospel points out that this is referring to the martyrdom of Peter. No doubt about that, but I wonder if Jesus is also trying to make a statement about the rest of Peter's life. Remember that Peter had just tried to return to his former life of fishing. In his confusion, not knowing what to make of the crucifixion and this whole idea of the resurrection, Peter wanted to go back to what he already knew: fishing. Jesus, on the shoreline, is impressing upon Peter the demands of love that go beyond what is familiar and comfortable. He says in effect, "Peter, you don't really have a choice here; if you're going to love me, then you must go and be a missionary, even if you're more comfortable on the boat." Love compels us to leave behind what is easy and comfortable and to do what love demands—what is best for others.

Isn't this true for us too? When we feel confused, lonely, nervous, or frightened, we want to go back to what is familiar. Jesus is saying, to Peter and to us, "Those days are over for you; don't go backwards into the past. Now you are compelled by love to go forth and feed my lambs and feed my sheep."

Recall the strange little detail that, upon recognizing the Lord, Peter first put on some clothes before he jumped into the water. When you and I go swimming, we usually remove a few layers of clothes before jumping into the water, which certainly would be true for the Israelites as well. So why did Peter put on an extra layer before jumping in? We know by now that every detail in John's Gospel is important, so what could this signify? It could be that Peter's very clothes signified his choice of direction in life. He had quite literally taken off the mantle of an apostle and was dressed only in the outfit of a fisherman. Fishermen in Israel would have worn just a very small type of loincloth. Perhaps John is trying to say that, once Peter recognizes Jesus, he immediately puts back on his robe of discipleship, his mantle of mission. In jumping into the water, then, he's leaving the boat behind once again. He's abandoning his nets, just as, long ago, when Jesus first called them, Peter and the disciples "left their nets and followed him" (Matthew 4:20). By choosing to go fishing, Peter had stepped back into his old life before Jesus, but now he's remembering who he is in Christ. Jesus makes sure Peter understands: he is now a missionary, no longer going after fish but sheep.

Finally, while the text doesn't say it explicitly, Jesus seems to stand up and start walking away when he says, "Follow me" (John 21:19). They were having this beautiful fish fry on the shore—you can imagine the picnic blanket spread out, and all of the fish and the drinks are laid upon it. And all of a sudden, Jesus says, "Follow me," gets up, and starts to walk. Everybody is scrambling; they're putting away the supplies, folding the picnic blanket, and trying to catch up to Jesus. Then Peter looks over at John and says, "Lord, what about him? What's going to happen to him?" And Jesus replies, in effect, "Don't worry about him. That's none of your business! What if I want him to have a completely different mission? You, follow me." And then he seems to walk on, and they have to catch up to Jesus.

Let's put all this together now. Jesus seems to be saying at least four important things to Peter in this story.

First, don't go back to the past. Peter's old profession, his old ways, and his old comforts are no longer the way. Jesus is now the way. Peter must stay a disciple; he must keep his missionary apparel on and live out the mission for which Jesus is sending him—even when it's uncomfortable.

Second, there's no room for self-loathing. Jesus doesn't allow Peter to wallow in his sin, so he takes him to confession and gives him absolution. He does this to heal him and also to help Peter to get over himself, so that he can go forward and be a good missionary.

Third, don't compare yourself to others. In turning Peter's gaze away from John and back to Jesus, he instructs Peter, "Don't worry about other people. I want you to follow me. Don't look to the side or to this person or that person; keep your eyes on me."

Fourth, and perhaps most surprisingly, Jesus is also saying no to an exclusive "Jesus and me" relationship. Of course, we do have an intimate, one-on-one relationship with Jesus. We belong to Jesus and Jesus belongs to us, but is it really exclusive in the end? No, it's always bursting outward. The disciples are not going to sit on the seashore for very long. Jesus has this intimate moment with them on the shore; it is quiet, peaceful, and exclusively theirs to enjoy. But then he stands up suddenly and says, "Let's go forward," and they all have to follow along. Not for long will they sit around and sing songs by the campfire. They have work to do.

So what about us? Like St. Peter and the others, as we celebrate and reflect upon the resurrection, we can sit on the seashore and enjoy the quiet, intimate moments with the resurrected Lord, but we're also going to hear Jesus prod us forward into mission. As Jesus told Peter, so he tells each of us to get over our self-loathing, to get ourselves reconciled with God in whatever way that takes, to let go of the past, to stop resorting back to things that are comfortable, to stop comparing ourselves to others, and, ultimately, after we have had our prayer time with Jesus alone in our room, to stand up and go do our missionary work.

We are on Day 28 of a thirty-day retreat, so perhaps Jesus is starting to prod us forward a bit more right now. Maybe Jesus is pushing us to begin to stand up from the seashore of this intimate time we've had together, to compel us outward to the world where we can feed our sheep.

Let's close with our passage once more.

Closing Prayer

When they had finished breakfast, Jesus said to Simon Peter, "Simon, son of John, do you love me more than these?" He said to him, "Yes, Lord, you know that I love you." He said to him, "Feed my lambs." He then said to him a second time, "Simon, son of John, do you love me?" He said to him, "Yes, Lord, you know that I love you." He said to him, "Tend my sheep." He said to him the third time, "Simon, son of John, do you love me?" Peter was distressed that he had said to him a third time, "Do you love me?" and he said to him, "Lord, you know everything; you know that I love you." [Jesus] said to him, "Feed my sheep. Amen, amen, I say to you, when you were younger, you used to dress yourself and go where you wanted; but when you grow old, you will stretch out your hands, and someone else will dress you and lead you where you do not want to go." He said this signifying by what kind of death he would glorify God. And when he had said this, he said to him, "Follow me."

Peter turned and saw the disciple following whom Jesus loved, the one who had also reclined upon his chest during the supper. . . . When Peter saw him, he said to Jesus, "Lord, what about him?" Jesus said to him, "What if I want him to remain until I come? What concern is it of yours? You follow me." (John 21:15-2-, 21-22)

Amen.

Day 29

The Fourth Week

Bible Passage: Acts 1:6-12

Welcome to Day 29 of *Ascending with Ignatius*. Today we will reflect on the Scripture passage of the Ascension: Acts 1:6-12.

Opening Prayer

In the name of the Father and of the Son and of the Holy Spirit.

When they had gathered together they asked him, "Lord, are you at this time going to restore the kingdom to Israel?" He answered them, "It is not for you to know the times or seasons that the Father has established by his own authority. But you will receive power when the holy Spirit comes upon you, and you will be my witnesses in Jerusalem, throughout Judea and Samaria, and to the ends of the earth." When he had said this, as they were looking on, he was lifted up, and a cloud took him from their sight. While they were looking intently at the sky as he was going, suddenly two men dressed in white garments stood beside them. They said, "Men of Galilee, why are you standing there looking at the sky? This Jesus who has been taken up from you into heaven will return in the same way as you have seen him going into heaven." Then they returned to Jerusalem from the mount called Olivet, which is near Jerusalem, a sabbath day's journey away. (Acts 1:6-12)

Amen.

Reflection

It's difficult to understand or even to imagine this extraordinary claim that our bodies, not just our souls, are to undergo resurrection and ascension into heaven. Perhaps it's not too extraordinary to believe in Jesus ascending, body and soul, into heaven, even though it's difficult to picture; Jesus is divine after all. But it gets a bit more difficult when we think about Mary being assumed body and soul, and it gets practically impossible to think of ourselves being resurrected in our physical bodies and ascending to heaven. And yet the Catholic Church is firm on this. As a matter of fact, we all say it every time we recite the Apostles Creed: "I believe in . . . the resurrection of the body and life everlasting." What does this mean? Does it mean that we somehow go back into our pre-dead bodies (which, as we know, begin to deteriorate after death)? Are we going to get to request which body we have—our teenage body when we were lean, healthy and vibrant; our pudgy midlife body; or maybe our deteriorating elderly body? That's just one question that arises with this strange belief of our bodies resurrecting and ascending into heaven.

Though we don't talk about it very much or perhaps even think about it, I have come to really love this belief. I'll explain why, but first I think it's important to help us a bit with our confusion. How does the resurrection of the body work, logistically? The short answer is simple: we don't know. But it helps to remember that Jesus' resurrected body both *was* and *was not* like his pre-resurrected body. Just like before his death, he has a real physical body. He eats a meal on the seashore and invites Thomas to touch his wounds, so we know his body was fleshly and physical.

Yet it was also different from before. Jesus was difficult to recognize by the people who had been with him for years; they thought he was a gardener or just another guy walking on a road to Emmaus or a sunbather on the seashore. And though his body is physical, it also seems to have some beyond-physical characteristics. Jesus goes through the locked doors of the Upper Room. He seems to appear and disappear at times, and then, in the ascension, he floats away into the air, vanishing behind a cloud. My point is that you and I have no idea what a resurrected body looks and feels like. We just don't know. We've never seen one; we've never touched one; we've never walked around in one. And Jesus would have us not think too hard about it because we're probably not able to comprehend exactly what's in the mind of God here.

In fact, in the ascension story we just read, the disciples even ask Jesus about some logistics of what he's going to do next, and Jesus answers in effect, "It's not for you to know; don't worry about that." A Jesuit friend of mine says that's a management issue, and we're in sales. Our job is to sell the resurrected Christ to all the world, so let's not worry too much about what the resurrected body will look and feel like. Let's let the Lord work out those details.

But then why is this belief in the bodily resurrection and ascension important at all? Why am I making such a fuss about this belief that we don't talk much about nor really understand? It's important because of the theological message behind it: God loves every inch of us.

God loves our souls, of course, and he loves our minds, but God also loves our bodies. God loves all of us completely and divinely, and he loves our bodies as much as he loves our souls. Since God loves every inch of us, of course God would want it all to be resurrected. That's an important thing to think about. What about you? Do you love your body as much as your soul? Probably not. We often have a lot of issues with our bodies. Everyone has things they don't like about their bodies, so it's easier to think about our souls ascending while we shed our bodies; but God loves every inch of us.

God loves every inch of creation too. Remember in the creation story in Genesis 1 and 2, we see God delighting over his marvelous creation, saying, "It is good." And the Book of Revelation tells us that God wants to lift up "a new heaven and a new earth" (21:1). God wants every leaf, every grain of sand, every feather of a bird—all of it—to be resurrected; it's all going to be in the new heaven and the new earth because God loves every inch of us. Remember that the resurrection is God restoring us to the Garden of Eden where, according to Genesis, God walked with us in the breezy times of the day, and we were naked and unashamed. God is restoring us back to the original beauty of our bodies and all of creation, so that there is nothing, no inch of us, that we need to be ashamed of anymore.

The Ascension, then, is not just a celebration of Jesus ascending into heaven. It's a celebration of the fact that God will restore all of creation, that we will have a new heaven and a new earth, and that God will love, restore, and use every inch of us. God will use our victories, but God will use our failures as well. God will save our souls, but God will restore our bodies as well.

Let us close, as always, with our Scripture passage.

Closing Prayer

When they had gathered together they asked him, "Lord, are you at this time going to restore the kingdom to Israel?" He answered them, "It is not for you to know the times or seasons that the Father has established by his own authority. But you will receive power when the holy Spirit comes upon you, and you will be my witnesses in Jerusalem, throughout Judea and Samaria, and to the ends of the earth." When he had said this, as they were looking on, he was lifted up, and a cloud took him from their sight. While they were looking intently at the sky as he was going, suddenly two men dressed in white garments stood beside them. They said, "Men of Galilee, why are you standing there looking at the sky? This Jesus who has been taken up from you into heaven will return in the same way as you have seen him going into heaven." Then they returned to Jerusalem from the mount called Olivet, which is near Jerusalem, a sabbath day's journey away. (Acts 1:6-12)

Amen.

Day 30

The Fourth Week

Bible Passages: John 16:5-22; Acts 2:1-13;
2 Corinthians 3:17-18

Congratulations! You've arrived at the final day of this thirty-day retreat, *Ascending with Ignatius*. You have ascended up the Mount of Olives with Jesus and St. Ignatius. From here we are ready to relish the mystery of Jesus ascending into heaven, and what that might mean for us as we move forward in our lives. Today let us reflect on three Scripture passages: John 16:5-22; Acts 2:1-13; and 2 Corinthians 3:17-18.

We begin with excerpts from John 16 as our opening prayer.

Opening Prayer

In the name of the Father and of the Son and of the Holy Spirit.

[Jesus said to his disciples,]

"But now I am going to the one who sent me. . . . But because I told you this, grief has filled your hearts. But I tell you the truth, it is better for you that I go. For if I do not go, the Advocate will not come to you. But if I go, I will send him to you. . . .

"A little while and you will no longer see me, and again a little while later and you will see me. . . . Amen, amen, I say to you, you will weep and mourn, while the world rejoices; you will grieve, but your grief will become joy. When a woman is in labor, she is in anguish because her hour has arrived; but when she has given birth to a child, she no longer remembers the pain because of her joy that a child has been born into the world. So you also are now in anguish. But I will see you again, and your hearts will rejoice, and no one will take your joy away from you." (John 16:5, 6-7, 16, 20-22)

Amen.

Reflection

These words come from Jesus' farewell discourses in John's Gospel just before his passion and death. As we saw on Day 26, scholars think that these farewell discourses could just as well fit immediately prior to the Ascension. Today's passage is a great example. Jesus tells them that after a time of not seeing him, during which they will grieve, they will once again be joyfully reunited with Jesus. This could refer to his death and resurrection, but placed before the Ascension, it also makes sense, as if Jesus were saying, "I have to ascend now. I have to go up to heaven, but a little while later, I will be with you again on Pentecost, when the Holy Spirit comes. Then your joy will be complete."

All of us want to ascend because that is our ultimate destiny and the Lord's will for us. The Lord wants us all to ascend, body and soul, into heaven. But even before that, right now, the Lord wants us to ascend from one plane to a higher plane. The Lord calls us to ascend again and again to a higher understanding of God. The Lord is always calling us to ascend to the next level of relationship with Jesus and with our fellow women and men. But this ascending comes at a cost. Jesus points out the anguish and grief involved; we do not want to let go of what we already have in order to get to the higher plane. We see this pattern with the disciples.

I have an amusing thought when I think about the Ascension. I think about the disciples not wanting to let Jesus go, and as Jesus starts to ascend, I imagine them grabbing onto his feet, trying to hold on to him as if he were a helium balloon. Of course, that didn't happen; they had the grace to let Jesus go. But I wonder if, in their hearts, they wanted to hold on to Jesus, whom they had come to know and love. In order to receive the Advocate, Jesus said in effect, "I have to leave you. You have to let me go. You cannot cling to me." He said the same thing to Mary Magdalene: "Do not cling to me because I need to ascend to the Father." Here in the farewell discourse, Jesus gives the same message to the disciples. Though their grief will be great right now, they must let him go so that he can send them the Holy Spirit.

Why was it necessary for Jesus to ascend in order to become present to them in a new way through the Holy Spirit? Jesus, in bodily form, was contained in one physical human body. He had one face, one voice, one language; but Jesus desired to come through his Holy Spirit so that he could have every face and speak in every language. That is indeed what we see in Pentecost when the Holy Spirit comes. Would that have been able to happen had the disciples not let go of Jesus' feet?

This is Jesus' message for you and me too. In order for us to receive the Spirit in our lives—to receive a bigger and broader manifestation of God's presence—then we must let go of the Jesus we've grown comfortable with. We have to let go of today's Jesus, if you will, in order to receive a greater Jesus, a greater manifestation of God's presence. In the same chapter from John's Gospel, Jesus says, "I have much more to tell you, but you cannot bear it now" (16:12). Jesus has this longing to come to us in bigger and greater ways, in deeper manifestations of his very self. But in order for you and me to receive this gift, we must let go. We must not cling to the Jesus that we've known in the past.

I'd like to share just one example from my own life. I grew up in Church Point, a small town in Louisiana. We had a wonderful but isolated existence in this small town. I knew Jesus, but I knew him in a very small way because I had such a small context. I didn't have a big and broad experience of life, and so my Jesus, if you will, was quite small. He was big enough for me in my one town, with my one culture of the people that I grew up with who looked like me, who saw things the way I saw them, and who spoke the same language I spoke. My Jesus was big enough for all of that.

But once I joined the Jesuits, I needed a bigger Jesus. I needed to let go of the Jesus I knew so that I could receive a bigger manifestation of Christ—one that could speak every language and wear multiple faces. This greater manifestation would allow me to go around the world and encounter Jesus, pointing him out like we are called to do. But none of this would have happened had I clung to my smaller Jesus—to my old manifestation of the Lord.

The Jesuits were quite good at teaching me about a bigger Jesus. It is an important aspect of Jesuit spirituality to let go of the things of yesterday so that we can receive what the Lord wants for us today. As St. Ignatius puts it, we are always to seek the *greater* glory of God. This word "greater" is the Latin word *magis*, so we say that we are always seeking the *magis*. We are always trying to ascend spiritually, and in order to do that, we must be ready to let go of what we already have. This is why Pope Benedict XVI, when he visited the Jesuits in Rome, said that our mission was to the frontiers. The Jesuit mission is to always seek out Jesus on the frontiers, to leave the old familiar land and venture into *terra incognita*—"unknown lands." In unknown lands, we can encounter a new manifestation of Christ Jesus and we can present that new manifestation to the Church and to the world.

This is why, at the end of the Spiritual Exercises, St. Ignatius has the beautiful *Suscipe* prayer. It begins, "Take, Lord. and receive all my liberty, my memory, and my understanding." Why do we give up our memory and our understanding? Because these are formed in the past. We let these things go so that we can receive a new manifestation of Christ. Here, at the end of the retreat, we ask ourselves: Are we tethered to the Jesus that we knew before the retreat, or are we ready to receive a new manifestation of Jesus? Do we exit this retreat with the same Jesus we entered with? If we do, then what was the point of the retreat after all? Indeed, the Lord is calling us to receive him in a new manifestation. Let him send his Spirit upon you in a new way. This is our calling. This is what Jesus asks us to do—to let go of the Jesus we knew in order to receive our new manifestation of Jesus.

So the end of the Spiritual Exercises is in fact a new beginning, just as the end of Jesus' life, death, resurrection, and ascension was a new beginning through Pentecost. Like the apostles and disciples, we receive the Holy Spirit of Christ and are sent out to feed his sheep.

My friends, before we go our separate ways and become the salt of the earth and the light of the world for all of the people that we encounter, let us close with the very words of St. Ignatius at the end of the Spiritual Exercises.

Closing Prayer

Take, Lord, and receive all my liberty,
my memory, and my understanding,
and my entire will,
All that I have and call my own.

You have given all to me.
To you, Lord, I return it.

Everything is yours; do with it what you will.
Give me only your love and your grace,
that is enough for me.[9]

Amen.

Notes

1. Henri J. M. Nouwen, *The Wounded Healer: Ministry in Contemporary Society* (New York: Doubleday, 1979), 72.
2. Pope Francis, *The Name of God Is Mercy* (New York: Random House, 2016), 70.
3. USCCB, "The Exsultet: The Proclamation of Easter," https://www.usccb.org/prayer-and-worship/liturgical -year-and-calendar/easter/easter-proclamation -exsultet.
4. Julian of Norwich, *All Will Be Well* (Notre Dame, IN: Quest Associates, 2008), 25.
5. Robert Llewelyn, *All Shall Be Well; The Spirituality of Julian of Norwich for Today* (New York: Paulist Press, 1985), 130-131.
6. Pope Francis, *The Infinite Tenderness of God: Meditations on the Gospels* (Frederick, MD: The Word Among Us Press, 2016), 32.

7. Gerald O'Connell, "Pope Francis: The Pandemic Has Given Us a Chance to Develop New Ways of Living," *America* (September 2, 2020), https://www.americamagazine.org/faith/2020/09/01/pope-francis-covid-19-pandemic-climate-change-cancel-debt.

8. St. Ignatius of Loyola, Louis J. Puhl, SJ, ed., *The Spiritual Exercises of St. Ignatius* (Westminster, MD: The Newman Press, 1951), 96.

9. St. Ignatius of Loyola, "Suscipe," Loyola Press, https://www.loyolapress.com/catholic-resources/prayer/traditional-catholic-prayers/saints-prayers/suscipe-prayer-saint-ignatius-of-loyola/.